Scot land the best

PETER IRVINE

exclusive edition for
SCOTLAND*on*SUNDAY

Author and journalist Pete Irvine is also Scotland's leading-edge event organizer. His company, Unique Events, created Edinburgh's annual Hogmanay Programme in 1993 (the year that he started *Scotland the Best*); it has become the world's biggest New Year's celebration. He is also the director of Scotland's annual contemporary-art gathering, the Glasgow Art Fair, and of The Outsider, Scotland's first environment and music festival.

In 2000 he received the Silver Thistle Award for his 'outstanding contribution to the development of tourism in Scotland' and the MBE for services to Edinburgh.

This edition has been produced exclusively for *Scotland on Sunday* by Collins, an imprint of
HarperCollinsPublishers
77-85 Fulham Palace Road
London W6 8JB

www.collins.co.uk

This edition published in 2008
Text © Peter Irvine 2008

The author asserts the moral right to be identified as the author of this work

ISBN 978-0-00-782251-5

Material extracted from *Scotland the Best* published by Collins in 2007
ISBN 978-0-00-725888-8
Text © Peter Irvine 2007

Designed and typeset by The Printer's Devil, Glasgow

Printed in Great Britain by
Clays Ltd, St Ives plc

A recent slogan called Scotland the 'best small country in the world'. I can confirm after my journey researching the new edition of *Scotland the Best* that it's not so small (consider its jagged, island-studded outline), but also that in many respects the word 'best' is not inappropriate.

Since the last edition, we have a new government and perhaps a new optimism and from my own determined investigations, I feel it's true to say that Scotland is very much on the up. Everywhere hotels, restaurants and bars are better, the restaurant culture of Edinburgh and Glasgow continues to flourish and some places like Skye and Inverness have improved dramatically. In these latter cases, this may partly be due to the emergence of the Highlands as a region both diverse and dynamic rather than just wild and pretty. Activity tourism has proliferated and from Fort William ('the UK Outdoor Capital') to the new festival, The Outsider, which I have a hand in, there is a new awareness that it is cool to be outdoors and Scotland is a rich, natural playground.

Space – or the lack of it – dictates that while this little edition gives a flavour of the book, much has to be omitted. This doesn't just mean entries themselves: ways of navigating the pages as you travel the country – notably by maps and by cross-references, which can tell you, for example, about a good pub in the area while you're out on your walk – haven't crossed over from the main book.

Scotland the Best is not a book about all the options – it only registers and recommends the best of what there is in its various categories. There is no mention of the mediocre even if it's all there is. This principle applies to natural features as well as to areas of human endeavour that are of interest to visitors and tourists. This range of interests continues to grow and is recognised in the new edition with new sections. With every edition, I like to think I get closer to the truth, closer to the perfect picture of how Scotland is at present.

Pete Irvine
Edinburgh, March 2008

The Ticks

All places listed here are notable in some way; those which are outstanding have been 'awarded' a tick.

 Amongst the very best in Scotland

 Amongst the best (of its type) in the UK

 Amongst the best (of its type) in the world, or simply unique

Listings generally are not in an order of merit although if there is one outstanding item it will always be at the top of the page and this obviously includes anything which has been given a tick.

The Hotel Codes

Tel TV shows that there are direct-dial telephones and TVs respectively in the bedrooms.

No Pets indicates that the hotel does not generally accept pets.

No Kids does not necessarily mean that children are not welcome, only that special provisions or rates are not usually made. Check by phone.

Rates are per person per night and should be used only to give an impression of cost. They are based on 2007 prices.

The Restaurant Codes

LO means last orders at the kitchen.

10pm/10.30pm means usually 10pm Mon-Fri, 10.30pm at weekends.

The Walk & Cycling Codes

Walks have the following codes: eg, *2-10km CIRC BIKE 1-A-1*

2-10km means the walk(s) may vary in length from 2km to 10km.

CIRC means the walk can be circular; *XCIRC* is not.
BIKE indicates a path suitable for ordinary bikes; *XBIKE* means unsuitable for cycling; *MTBIKE* means suitable for mountain bikes.

The *1-A-1* Code:
The first number shows how easy the walk is. *1* is easy; *2* is medium difficulty, e.g. standard hillwalking; and *3* is difficult: preparation and map needed.

A, B or C shows how easy it is to find the path. *A*: easy; *B*: not obvious, but you'll get there; *C*: map and preparation or guide needed).

The last number (*1, 2 or 3*) shows required footwear. *1*: ordinary shoes, including trainers, are probably okay unless the ground is very wet; *2*: walking boots are needed; *3*: wear serious walking or hiking boots.

Part 1

Scotland the best

Wha's Like Us?

Wemyss Bay-Rothesay Ferry

CalMac
01475 650100

Wemyss Bay's glass-roofed station (60km from Glasgow on the A78) is redolent of an age-old terminus; the frequent ferry has all the Scottish traits and sausage rolls you can handle; and Rothesay with its period mansions appears like a gentle water-colour from holidays past. Visit its Victorian toilet and Mount Stuart. Both are superb.

Loch Etive Cruises

01866 822430,
though booking
not essential.
Easter-mid Oct.
Leaves 12-2pm
(not Sat).

From Taynuilt (Oban 20km) through the narrow waters of atmospheric Loch Etive for 3 hours. The pier is 2km from Taynuilt crossroads on the A85. Also **Loch Shiel Cruises** (01687 470322), leaving from near Glenfinnan House Hotel on the Road to the Isles, the A830, offer various trips on glorious Loch Shiel.

Glenelg-Kylerhea

01599 522273
Apr-Oct
(frequent)
9am-6pm (7pm
in summer). Also
Sun in summer
9am-6pm.

The shorter of the 2 ferry trips to Skye, and the best way to get there if you're not pushed for time. The drive to Glenelg from the A87 is spectacular and so is this five-minute crossing of the deep Narrows of Kylerhea. Otter-watch hide at Kylerhea.

Corran Ferry

01855 841243
Contin till
8.50pm summer,
7.50pm winter.
Later at week-
ends.

From Ardgour to Nether Lochaber across the narrows of Loch Linnhe, a convenient five-minute crossing to points south of Mallaig takes you to the wildernesses of Moidart and Ardnamurchan. A charming, fondly regarded journey in its own right.

Maid of the Forth to Inchcolm Island

0131 331 4857
1 hour 30 minutes
ashore. Mar-Oct.

The wee boat (though they say it holds 225 people) leaves daily at different times from Hawes Pier in South Queensferry opposite the Hawes Inn, just under the famous railway bridge, and from Newhaven Harbour in town. Phone for times. 45-minute trips under the bridge and on to pretty Inchcolm Island with walks, an impressive ruined abbey, birdlife and seals.

The *Waverley*

0845 130 4647

'The World's Last Sea-going Paddle Steamer' plied the Clyde in the glorious 'Doon the Water' days and is *the* way to see the West Coast. Sailings are from Glasgow's Anderson Quay (or Greenock or Ayr) to Rothesay, Kyles of Bute and Arran.

The West Highland Line

08457 484950
Glasgow Queen
Street-Mallaig:
3 trains daily;
5 hours

One of Europe's most picturesque rail journeys and the best way to get to Skye from the south. Travel to Fort William from Glasgow then relax and watch the stunning scenery go by. Viaducts (including the Harry Potter one) and tunnels over loch and down dale.

Two Rail Journeys from Inverness

08457 484950
Inverness-Kyle of
Lochalsh: 3 trains
daily; 2 hours 30
minutes

Inverness-Wick:
3 trains daily in
summer; 3 hours
50 minutes

To Kyle of Lochalsh and to Wick: both are mesmerising. For the former, get a window seat and take an atlas: the last section through Glen Carron and around the coast at Loch Carron is especially fine. Inverness-Wick takes longer. The section skirting the east coast from Lairg-Helmsdale is full of drama, followed by the transfixing monotony of the Flow Country.

The Plane to Barra

0870 8509850
12-seater Otter
lands and leaves
daily according to
the tide

BA's Glasgow-Barra flight is special not just for the other islands it passes over, but because Barra's airport is on Cockleshell Beach (11 km from Castlebay) after a splendid approach.

Part 2

Particular Places To Stay, Eat & Drink

The Three Chimneys

Colbost, Skye
01470 511258
8 rooms
Tel TV £85+

www.thethreechimneys.co.uk
7km west of Dunvegan to Glendale on B884. Rooms across from the great Three Chimneys restaurant in the recently freshened The House Over-by, within sight and smell of the sea. Split-level rooms with own doors to the sward. A model of its kind, sooften full. Book for dinner!

The Barley Bree

Muthill near Crieff
01764 681451
5 rooms TV
£38-45

www.barleybree.com
Instant hit from summer '07: stylish, excellent value, great food, tasteful and comfortable rooms. Must be the French connection (chef Fabrice Bouteloup). Bar/restaurant open for lunch and dinner (closed Mon).

Glenelg Inn

Glenelg
01599 522273
6 rooms
+1 cottage
£38-45

www.glenelg-inn.com
Almost at the end of that great road over the hill from Shiel Bridge on the A87 is this civilised hostelry. Decent food (Tue-Sat), good drinking, snug lounge. Garden with tables and views. Charming rooms. From Glenelg, take the best route to Skye.

Argyll Hotel

Iona
01681 700334
16 rooms
Mar-Nov
£38-45

www.argyllhoteliona.co.uk
On a beautiful, turquoise bay on the road between ferry and abbey. Daytrippers come and go but stay! A charming hotel and a remarkable island. Cosy rooms, good food fresh from the organic garden. The real peace and quiet. Nice for kids.

Kilberry Inn

Nr Tarbert, Argyll
01880 770223
3 rooms TV
Mar-Dec £38-45

www.kilberryinn.com
Halfway round the Knapdale peninsula on the B8024. Homely inn with simple, inexpensive rooms and excellent cooking. Michelin Bib Gourmand '07. A gem.

Craw Inn

Auchencrow
01890 761253
3 rooms
£30-38

www.thecrawinn.co.uk
5 km A1 and well worth short detour into Berwickshire countryside. Quintessential inn with cosy pub, dining room. Funky furniture, simple rooms. Food decent, wines extraordinary. Lunch and dinner.

The Stein Inn

Waternish, Skye
01470 592362
5 rooms
£30 or less

www.stein-inn.co.uk
Off B886 the Dunvegan-Portree road, about 10km Dunvegan, in a row of cottages on waterside. The 'oldest inn on Skye' with great pub (open fire, good grub) and comfortable small rooms. Great value in a special spot. Excellent seafood restaurant adjacent.

Plockton Hotel

Plockton
01599 544274
11 rooms
Tel TV No pets
£38-45

www.plocktonhotel.com
On the shoreline of one of Scotland's most picturesque villages. With many visitors, this pub gets busy but the food is great and rooms upstairs are recently refurbished and not without charm.

West Loch Hotel

Tarbert
01880 820283
8 rooms TV
£38-45

www.westlochhotel.co.uk
By A83 west of Tarbert. An inexpensive stopover en route to the islands. Comfortably furnished; some original features. Board games and books dotted around, children welcome in relaxed, friendly atmosphere. New owners. Good value, but roadside rooms may be noisy.

Old Inn

Gairloch
01445 712006
17 rooms
Tel TV
£38-45

Southern approach on A832, tucked away by the river and 'old bridge'. Excellent pub for food, music (traditional and contemporary nights Tue/Fri). Nice, simple rooms. The pub goes like a fair. Routinely recommended in pub guides.

Cairnbaan Hotel

*Cairnbaan nr
Lochgilphead*
01546 603668
*12 rooms
Tel TV
£38-45*

www.cairnbaan.com
The main attraction here is the location overlooking lochs of the Crinan Canal – nice to watch or walk (all the way to Crinan) if not messing about on a boat yourself. Decent pub grub in or out; less successful dinner menu. Some ales.

Pier House

Port Appin
01631 730302
*12 rooms
Tel TV No Pets
£38-60*

www.pierhousehotel.co.uk
An inn at the end of the road (the minor road that leads off the A828 Oban to Fort William) and at the end of the 'pier', where the tiny passenger ferry leaves for Lismore. Bistro restaurant with decent seafood in great setting. Comfy motel-type rooms (the more expensive overlook the sea and island) and conservatory restaurant and lounge. Great place to take kids.

Glenisla Hotel

*Kirkton of
Glenisla*
01575 582223
*6 rooms
£38-45*

www.glenisla-hotel.com
20km northwest of Kirriemuir via B951 at head of this secluded story-book glen. A home from home: hearty food, real ale and local colour. Fishers, stalkers, trekkers and walkers all come by. Miles from the town literally and laterally. Neat rooms look into the countryside but could do with a wee makeover; convivial bar (sometimes live music).

Meikleour Hotel

Meikleour
01250 883206
*5 rooms TV
£45-60*

www.meikleour-inn.co.uk
Just off the A93 Perth-Blairgowrie road (on the B984) by and behind the famously high beech hedge (a Perthshire icon). Roadside inn with quiet accommodation and food in dining room or (more atmosphere) the bar. Refurbishment of rooms in progress.

Bridge of Orchy Hotel

Bridge of Orchy
01838 400208
10 rooms
+ bunkhouse
Tel TV
£38-45

www.bridgeoforchy.co.uk
Unmissable on the A82 (the road to Glencoe, Fort William and Skye) 11km north of Tyndrum. Old inn extensively refurbished and run as a stopover hotel. Simple, quite stylish rooms. A la carte menu and specials in pub/conservatory. Good spot for the malt or a munch on the West Highland Way. Food LO 9pm.

Cluanie Inn

Glenmoriston
01320 340238
12 rooms
+ bunkhouse
Tel
£30-38 / £45-60

www.cluanieinn.com
On main road to Skye 15km before Shiel Bridge, a traditional inn surrounded by the summits that attract walkers and travellers: the Five Sisters, the Ridge and the Saddle. Inn rooms can be high-spec – one with sauna, one with jacuzzi! Bar food LO 9pm. Bunkhouse basic. Friendly staff.

The Kames Hotel

Tighnabruaich
01700 811489
10 rooms TV
£38-45

www.kames-hotel.com
Frequented by passing yachtsmen who moor alongside and pop in for lunch. Good base for all things offshore; marine cruises or a nostalgic journey on a 'puffer', with a great selection of malts to warm you up before or after. Hotel recently taken over by enterprising and tasteful threesome so it all looks lovely now: calming neutral colours, simply stylish. Food LO in bar 9pm.

Gordon Inn

Yarrow
01750 82222
10 rooms
+ bunkhouse
£30-38

www.thegordonarmsyarrow.com
Old Borders coaching inn at historic crossroads deep in James Hogg country – there's a letter above the mantelpiece. Recent refurbishment has brought this place to a comfortable as well as cosy standard. Reasonable accommodation and decent meals (till 9/10pm).

The Ceilidh Place

Ullapool
01854 612103
23 rooms Tel
£60-85 /
£30 or less

www.ceilidhplace.com
Jean Urquhart's place encapsulates traditional Scottish culture and hospitality, interpreted in a contemporary manner. It caters for all sorts with an excellent hotel above; bistro/bar below (occasional live ceilidh-style music); bunkhouse; and a bookshop. Scottish-ness is all here and nothing embarrassing in sight.

The Albannach

Lochinver
01571 844407
5 rooms Tel
Mar-Dec
£38-45

www.thealbannach.co.uk
2km outside Lochinver on A837, at the bridge. Lovely 18th-century house in scenic Assynt, where the mountains can take your breath away even without going up them. The outbuilding overlooking the croft gives extra privacy and space. Some gorgeous suites. Unwind in tasteful, informal surroundings. Food is best for miles.

Ballachullish House

Ballachullish
01855 811266
8 rooms
Tel No Pets
£60-85

www.ballachullishhouse.com
On A828 to Oban; not to be confused with the nearby Ballachulish Hotel. The house is through a charming golf course. Ballachulish is Michelin-rated in the top fine-dining rooms in Scotland and is a west-of-Scotland destination. House makes much of its historical background (Appin murder, Glencoe etc) and tasteful update of 17th-century laird's lair.

Kildrummy Castle Hotel

Near Alford
01975 571288
16 rooms
Feb-Dec
Tel TV
£85+

www.kildrummycastlehotel.co.uk
60km west of Aberdeen via A944 lies this comfortable chunk of Scottish Baronial in a spectacular location in the green Don valley with real Highlands aura. Well placed if you're on the 'Castle Trail'. The redolent ruins of Kildrummy Castle stand

on the opposite bluff and a gorgeful of gardens between. Some rooms small, but all very Scottish. Romantic in autumn when the gardens are good. Jacket and tie for dinner.

Eilean Iarmain

✓

Skye
01471 833332
12 rooms
+ 4 suites
Tel TV
£60-85 / £85+

www.eilean-iarmain.co.uk
Sleat area on south of island, this snug gaelic inn nestles in the bay and is the classic island hostelry. A dram in your room awaits from the adjacent whisky company. Bedrooms in hotel are best but cottage annexe is quieter. New suites in adjacent steading more expensive but nice. Food real good in dining room or pub. Mystic shore walks. Very gaelic.

Glenfinnan House

✓

Glenfinnan
01397 722235
13+ rooms
Mar-Nov
£35-60

www.glenfinnanhouse.com
Off the Road to the Isles (A830 Fort William to Mallaig). Ongoing refurbishment retains its charm; the huge rooms remain intimate and cosy with open fires. Impromptu sessions and ceilidhs wherever there's a gathering in the bar. Solitude achievable in the huge grounds, or fishing or dreaming on Loch Shiel at the foot of the lawn (row boat and cruise boat nearby). Quintessential!

Savoy Park

Ayr
01292 266112
15 rooms
Tel TV
£38-45

www.savoypark.com
In an area of many indifferent hotels this one, owned and run by the Henderson family for over 40 years, is a real Scottish gem. Many weddings here. Period features, lovely garden, not too much tartan, but a warm, cosy, lived-in atmosphere. Round one of the fireplaces: 'blessed be God for his giftis'.

Monachyle Mhor

Nearr
Balquhidder
01877 384622
13 rooms
Tel TV
£45-85+

www.monachylemhor.com
Negotiate the thread of road by Loch Voil from Balquhidder (11km from the A84 Callander-Crianlarich). Farmhouse overlooks the loch from the magnificent Balquhidder Braes and was the first really cool boutique hotel in the Highlands. Ongoing refurbishment of rooms: contemporary, calm and sexy. Some in courtyard annexe; some cheaper; all very individual. Bar locals and visitors use. Friendly, cosy, not expensive; a place to relax summer or winter. Tastefully done.

Ardeonaig

Loch Tay
01567 820400
20 rooms
Tel
£45-85+

www.ardeonaighotel.co.uk
On narrow and scenic south Loch Tay road midway between Kenmore and Killin. An airy roadside inn by the water opposite Ben Lawers. South African chef/prop making the most of this perfectly remote location. Stylish rooms, great bar and excellent dining with top urban standard of service. And friendly! Upstairs library with cool books and a dreamy view of the Ben. Recent refurbishment. Love that loch!

The Torridon

Glen Torridon
near Kinlochewe
01445 791242
19 rooms
Tel TV
No kids No pets
£85+

www.lochtorridonhotel.com
Impressive former hunting lodge on lochside, surrounded by majestic mountains. A cosy, family-run baronial house with relaxed atmosphere, developing into a Highland 'experience' with activities like clay-pigeon shoots, mountain biking or fishing with guides. Lots of walking possibilities. This great hotel has spawned a cheaper travel lodge in the outdoors kind of option: The Torridon Inn in adjacent block with own bar and bistro. The budget choice (12 rooms) but dine in the hotel if you can.

Tiroran House

Isle of Mull
01681 705232
6 rooms
+ 2 cottages
Mar-Nov
TV No pets
£60-85

www.tiroran.com
Southwest corner of the island on road to Iona from Craignure, then B8035 round Loch na Keal. Family-friendly small country house in fabulous gardens by the sea, refurbished by inimitable owners Laurence Mackay and Katie Munro (Katie a Cordon Bleu cook). Near Iona and Ulva ferry; you won't miss Tobermory. Excellent food from sea and kitchen garden. Lovely rooms. Sea eagles fly over, otters in the bay.

Moor of Rannoch Hotel

Rannoch Station
01882 633238
5 rooms
Mid Feb-mid Nov
£38-45

www.moorofrannoch.co.uk
Beyond Pitlochry and the Trossachs and far west via Loch Tummel and Loch Rannoch (B8019 and B8846), so a wonderful journey to the edge of Rannoch Moor and adjacent station: you could get the sleeper from London and be here for breakfast. Four trains either way each day via Glasgow. Literally the end of the road but an exceptional find in the middle of nowhere. Cosy, wood-panelled rooms, great restaurant (open to non-residents). Quintessential Highland inn. Great walking.

Glen Clova Hotel

Near Kirriemuir
01575 550350
10 rooms
Tel TV
No pets
£38-45

www.clova.com
25km north of Kirriemuir to the head of the glen on B955; once you're there there's nowhere to go but up. Rooms all ensuite and surprisingly well appointed. Climbers' bar (till all hours). Superb walking hereabouts (eg Loch Brandy and the classic path to Loch Muick). A laid-back get-away though lots of families drive up for Sunday lunch. Also a (cheap) bunkhouse and two new 'luxury' lodges. Great value.

Corsewall Lighthouse Hotel

Near Stranraer
01776 853220
6 rooms
+ suites
Tel TV
£60-85

www.lighthousehotel.co.uk
Only 15 minutes from Stranraer (via A718 to Kirkcolm) and follow the signs, but way up on the peninsula and as it suggests a hotel made out of a working lighthouse. Romantic and offbeat, decent food too, and there are attractions nearby especially at Portpatrick 30 minutes away through the maze of quiet backroads.

Mackays

Durness
01971 511202
7 rooms
Apr-Oct
TV No pets
£38-45

www.visitmackays.com
Remote from the rest of Scotland (the top northwest corner) but actually in the centre of the township. Many interesting distractions nearby. Highland chic: a comfortable, contemporary restaurant with rooms. Wood and slate: the coolest retreat in the North. Great food.

Applecross Inn

Applecross
01520 744262
8 rooms
£30-38

www.applecross.uk.com/inn
At the end of the spectacular road over the Pass of the Cattle, north of Kyle of Lochalsh. This waterside inn is a haven of hospitality; it buzzes all seasons. Rooms small (1 and 7 best), finally all ensuite '07. Judy Fish and a great team and a real chef look after you. Poignant visitor centre, walled garden, lovely walks and even a real pizza hut in summer to keep you happy in Applecross for days.

Corriechoille Lodge

By Spean Bridge
01397 712002
5 rooms
Mar-Oct
TV No pets
£38-45

www.corriechoille.com
3km from south bridge via road by the station. A lovely road and spectacularly situated; it's great to arrive. Justin and Lucy share their perfect retreat with you in the house and two turf-covered chalets out back.

Glenmorangie House

Cadboll by Fearn
01862 871671
9 rooms Tel
No pets £60-85

www.theglenmorangiehouse.com
On the little peninsula east of Tain off the A9 (10km). Comfortable mansion once owned by the distillery, now by Louis Vuitton Moët Hennessy. Chef has a good reputation. Class not just in the glass.

Tomdoun Hotel

Near Invergarry
01809 511218
10 rooms
£38-45

www.tomdoun.com
20km from Invergarry, 12km off the A87 to Kyle of Lochalsh. This 19th-century coaching inn replaced a much older one; off the beaten track but perfect for fishing and walking (Loch Quoich and Knoydart, the last wilderness, have been waiting a long time for you). Superb views over Glengarry and Bonnie Prince Charlie's country. House-party atmosphere, mix-match furniture and nice dogs. Real chef with meticulously sourced seafood menu.

The Pier House

Inverie, Knoydart
01687 462347
4 rooms
Mar-Oct
£30 or less

www.pierhousehotel.co.uk
Currently the only restaurant on this far-away peninsula, though good grub at the pub nearby. Accessible on foot (sic) from Kinlochourn (25km) or Bruce Watt's boat from Mallaig (01687 462320). Friendly couple offer warm hospitality in their home and surprisingly good cooking for somewhere so remote; rovers do return.

Doune Stone Lodge

Knoydart
01687 462667
4 rooms
+ lodge
Apr-Sep
No pets
£38-45

www.doune-knoydart.co.uk/stlodge.html
As above, on remote Knoydart and this great spot on the western tip overlooks a bay on the Sound of Sleat. Their own boats pick you up from Mallaig and drop you round the inlets for walking. Otherwise 8km from Inverie. Rooms and lodge for 12. Own restaurant. Only lodge available in winter.

Tomich Hotel

Near Cannich
01456 415399
8 rooms
Tel TV
£38-45

www.tomichhotel.co.uk
8km from Cannich which is 25km from Drumnadrochit. Fabulous Plodda Falls are nearby. Cosy country inn in conservation village with added bonus of use of swimming pool in nearby steading. Faraway feel; surprising bar round the back where what's left of the locals do linger. Good base for outdoorsy weekend. Glen Affric across the way.

Shieldaig Lodge

Near Cannich
01445 741250
13 rooms
TV
£38-45

www.shieldaiglodge.com
South of Gairloch by A832 then out towards Redpoint on B8056, a beautiful drive. This hunting/shooting/mainly fishing hotel with a spectacular setting overlooking Loch Gairloch has old-style rooms and service so it's comfy to be in. Decent value. Badachro Inn nearby for grub or the Old Inn back in Gairloch. Big Victorian rooms at front are best.

ALSO ...
The Carnegie Club

✓ ✓ ✓

Skibo Castle,
Dornoch
01862 894600
21 rooms
11 lodges
Tel TV
No pets
£85+

www.carnegieclub.co.uk
Not a hotel, they stress, but you may want to check their website and join their waiting list. Mentioned here because it is top and it is in Scotland. A vast estate once home to the formidable Andrew Carnegie. The sumptuous castle retains its original furnishings (silk wallpaper, panelling, etc.) and the service from your discreet 'hosts' is exemplary. Lodges in the grounds offer more privacy, with the obligatory two golf courses, spa, gym, pool and 'beach', all oases of relaxing indulgence – vintage Rolls Royces take you around. Many dining options. Everything here has a plus factor, including the cost.

All these spas offer day visits and specific treatments.

One Spa

*The Sheraton
Grand Hotel,
Edinburgh
0131 229 9131*

www.one-spa.net
Unquestionably the best spa in the city; and on loads of national/international lists. And probably the best thing about the hotel which is centrally situated on Festival Sq. As well as the usual (but reasonably spacious) pool there's another one which extends outdoors dangling infinity-style over Conference Sq at the back of the hotel. Decent gym. Exotic hydrotherapy and a host of treatments. Day and half-day tickets available.

The Kohler Waters Spa

✓ ✓

*The Old Course
Hotel,
St Andrews
01334 474371*

www.oldcoursehotel.co.uk
In the lovely Old Course golfing resort, this beautifully designed leisure and treatment suite is just one of many reasons for staying. The gym looks out over the Old Course (and there's a roof-top hot tub). In the main suite the 20-metre pool, monsoon showers, saunas and crystal steam rooms are in a very calm and relaxing environment. 11 therapy rooms offer a vast range of treatments.

Stobo Castle

✓ ✓

*Stobo near
Peebles
01721 725300*

www.stobocastle.co.uk
Border baronial mansion 10km south of Peebles in beautiful countryside of towering trees and trickling burns. Mainly a hotel but day visits are possible; the spa is the heart of the whole pampering experience. Over 70 treatments. Not too much emphasis on exercise. Classic, standard rooms and suites; also lodge. Bespoke treatment for men and women. You do feel they know what they are doing; all medical peculiarities accounted for.

The Spa, Gleneagles Hotel

Auchterarder
01764 662231

www.gleneagles.com
The leisure suites at Gleneagles have always offered (obviously) one of the best spa experiences. In 2007 the spa was completely refurbished and relocated. Gleneagles offers Espa body treatments and uses all their oils and unguents. Treatments vary from the usual aromatherapy and facials to hot-stone therapy and Balinese and ayurvedic applications. All in superb surroundings.

The Spa, Isle of Eriska Hotel

Ledaig
01631 720371

www.eriska-hotel.co.uk
The Isle of Eriska ('hotel/spa/island'), one of Scotland's most comfy country-house hotels, is 20km north of Oban. Apart from the usual indulgences they have created (and are still developing at time of going to press) a lovely spa separate from the main building in the gardens overlooking the new golf course. There's a pool and gym a separate café with terrace and several treatment rooms using Espa products. Perfect tranquillity.

Yu Spa, Apex City Quay Hotel

Dundee
01382 309309

www.apexhotels.co.uk
The inexpensive and accessible spa is part of the overall offering at this central business hotel, most definitely the best in the city. A new build on the emerging waterfront with spa and swimming pool occupying a corner of the ground floor. Therapies combine the ethos and products from 'Elemis' in over 50 treatments for men and women. Japanese-inspired wooden hot tubs, herb infused steam room and sauna. Everything you need to do before you go out again and face Dundee.

The Spa, Marine Hotel

North Berwick
01620 897333

www.macdonaldhotels.co.uk
The spa in the newly renovated ('07) Marine Hotel which has been here forever overlooking the golf course. Salt-water hydro pool, aroma steam room, 'bio sauna', a 'cold therapy room' and a 'serenity relaxation room' all contribute to a well thought-out suite of facilities removed from the main hustle and bustle of the hotel. 'Decleor' products are offered in a wide range of treatments which includes a men's menu. All the usual beautifications; some exotica.

The Spa, Cameron House Hotel

Loch Lomond
01389 713659

www.devere.co.uk
The spa in the recently made over De Vere Cameron House Hotel and Golf Course on the banks of the loch. Spa inculcates the 'Kirsten Florien philosophy' which revolves around hydrotherapy, aromatherapy and thalassotherapy, balnotherapy and pelotherapy (whatever they are) with a host of products including the 'highly acclaimed, ageless Caviar Collection' (it says here). There's also a new skincare range called Carita. I don't know anything about these but there's a comprehensive booklet. There's a pool and a steam room and all the usual facilities including a 'rasul' chamber.

Caravan sites and camp grounds that are especially kid-friendly, with good facilities and a range of things to do (including a good pub). Key:

HIRE *Caravans for rent*
NO HIRE *No rental caravans available*
X CARAVAN *Number of caravan pitches*
X TENT *Number of tent pitches*
FLEXIBLE *They take caravans and tents according to demand.*

Glen More Camp Site

Near Aviemore
01479 861271
240 Tents
Dec-Oct
No Hire

9km from Aviemore on the road to the ski slopes, the B970. Across the road from the Glen More Visitor Centre and adjacent to the Loch Morlich Watersports Centre. Extensive grassy site on loch side with trees and views of the mountains. Loads of activities include watery ones especially the reindeer and at the Coylumbridge Hotel where there' s a pool and The Fun House – a separate building full of stuff to amuse kids of all ages (soft play, mini golf, etc). Well stocked shop at site entrance.

Applecross Campsite

Applecross
01520 744268
Flexible
Apr-Oct
No Hire

www.applecross.uk.com/campsite
First thing you come to as you approach the coast after your hair-raising drive over the *bealach*, the mountain pass. Grassy meadow in farm setting 1km sea. Usual facilities and Flower Tunnel bakery and café Apr-Oct till 9pm, till 5pm Mon and Tue. A green, grassy safe haven.

Shieling Holidays

✓

Craignure, Mull
01680 812496
80 Tents
30 Caravans
Apr-mid Oct
No Hire

www.shieldingholidays.co.uk
35km from Tobermory but right where the ferry comes in. Great views and a no-nonsense, thought-of-everything camp park. Self-catering 'shielings' (carpeted cottage tents with heaters and ensuite facilities) or hostel beds if you prefer.

Loads to do and see, including nearby Torosay and Duart Castles; the fun Mull Light Railway next door. Village inn and public swimming pool on the way.

Carfraemill Camping & Caravanning Site

Lauder
01578 750697
60 Tents
Mar-Oct
No Hire

www.campingandcaravanningclub.co.uk
Aka Lauder Camping & Caravanning Club. Just off A697 where it joins the A68 near Oxton. Small, sheltered and friendly campsite in the green countryside with trickling burn. Four chalets for hire on site. Good gateway to the Borders (Melrose 20km). The Lodge (or Jo's Kitchen as it is also known) adjacent has great family restaurant where kids made very welcome (play area and the food they like, etc).

Sands Holiday Centre

Gairloch
01455 712252
Many Tents
100 Caravans
Hire

www.highlandcaravancamping.co.uk
4km Gairloch (road to Melvaig) with views to the islands, a large park with dunes and its own sandy beach. Kids' play area but plenty to do and see in Gairloch itself – a great pub, the Old Inn, for adults. Well equipped shop, mountain bikes for hire; great camping in dunes plus walking, fishing, etc.

Boat of Garten Caravan Park

Boat of Garten
01479 831652
37 Tents
Hire

www.boatofgartenholidaypark.com
In the village itself, a medium-sized, slightly regimented site tailored to families with play area for the kids and even cots available to rent for the very wee. Cabins if the Scottish weather gets too much. Not the most rural or attractive site in the Highlands, but lots on the doorstep to keep the kids happy, including brilliant ie kid-brilliant Landmark Centre and Loch Garten ospreys.

Oban Divers Caravan park

Oban
01631 562755
32 Tents
30 Caravans
Mar-Oct
No Hire

www.obandivers.co.uk
1.5 miles out of Oban. Quiet, clean and friendly ground with stream running through. All sorts of 'extras' such as undercover cooking area, BBQ, adventure playground. No dogs. A good base for day trips including Rare Breeds Farm and Sealife Sanctuary.

Cashel Caravan & Campsite

Rowardennan
01360 870234
135 Tents
100 Caravans
Mar-Oct
No Hire

Forestry Commission site on the quieter shores of Loch Lomond in Queen Elizabeth Forest Park. Excellent facilities and tons to do in the surrounding area which includes Ben Lomond and plootering by the loch.

Balmeanach Park

Fishnish, Mull
01680 300342
Flexible
Apr-Oct
No Hire

Farm-like camp site on main road to Tobermory 1km from Lochaline (Ardnamurchan) Ferry. Sheltered, grassy site with café serving breakfast-dinner. Friendly, central, safe.

Sligachan

Skye
01478 650204
Flexible
Jan-Dec

The camp site you see at the major bend in the road on the A87 going north to Portree from the bridge and the ferries. Sligachan is major hotel landmark and its facilities include all-day bistro/Seumas' bar. Lovely site by river with many walks. Warden lives on site. Pitch up, check in.

Resipole Farm

Ardnamurchan
01478 650204
Flexible
Jan-Dec

www.resipole.co.uk
Arrive via Corran Ferry or from Mallaig or Fort William route via Lochailort. Extensive grassy landing on lochside with all mod cons including shop, dishwashers, mashing machines. Gorgeous Ardnamurchan all around you.

The selection listed here is of pubs outside the main cities: they have their own listings in Scotland the Best.

Drover's Inn

✓✓

Inverarnan

www.thedroversinn.co.uk

A famously Scottish drinking den/hotel on the edge of the Highlands just north of Ardlui at the head of Loch Lomond and 12km south of Crianlarich on the A82. Smoky, low-ceilinged rooms, open ranges, whisky in the jar, stuffed animals in the hall and kilted barmen; this is nevertheless the antithesis of the contrived Scottish tourist pub.

The Mishnish

✓✓

Tobermory

www.mishnish.co.uk

The family-run Mish has always been the real Tobermory. 7 days till late. Often live music from Scottish traditional to DJs and indie especially Sat. Different rooms, nooks and crannies. Great pub grub, open fire. Something, as they say, for everybody.

Old Forge

✓

Inverie, Knoydart
01687 462267

www.theoldforge.co.uk

A warm haven for visitors to this remote peninsula. Suddenly you're part of the community, real ales and real characters, excellent pub grub. Lunch and LO 9pm. Stay along the road at the brilliant guesthouse or bunk. (info@knoydart.org).

Clachaig Inn

✓

Glencoe
01855 811252

www.clachaig.com

Deep in the glen itself down the road signed off the A82, 5km from Glencoe village. Both the pub with its wood-burning stove and the lounge are woody and welcoming. Backdoor is best for muddy boots or those averse to leather-studded furniture. Real ale and real climbers and walkers. Handy for hostel 2km down road. Decent food (in bar/lounge) and good, inexpensive accommodation including 4 lodges. They have beer fests.

Tigh-An-Truish

Clachan,
Isle of Seil
01852 300242

www.tigh-an-truish.co.uk
Beside the much-photographed 'Bridge over the Atlantic' which links the 'Isle' of Seil with the 'mainland'. On B884, 8km from B816 and 22km south of Oban. Country pub with 2 apartments above (with views of the bridge). A place where no one cares how daft your hair looks after a hard day's messing about on boats. Food LO 8.30pm (Mar-Oct).

Castlebay Bar

Castlebay,
Barra
01852 300242

www.castlebay-hotel.co.uk
Adjacent to the Castlebay Hotel. A brilliant bar. All human life is here. This is more Irish than all the Irish makeovers to be found on the mainland. Occasional live music including The Vatersay Boys; conversations with strangers. New owners '07. Let's hope the spell is unbroken.

Taybridge Bar

129 Perth Road,
Dundee

Legendary drinking place. Established in 1867: the smoke-filled gloom of a Dundee afternoon. When Peter Howson runs out of Glaswegian gnarled heads, he might come here. Women are present, but usually accompanied by their 'man' or behind the bar listening to their views on the world outside.

Cluanie Inn

Loch Cluanie
01320 340238

www.cluanieinn.com
On A87 at head of Loch Cluanie 15km before Shiel Bridge on the long road to

Kyle of Lochalsh. A wayside inn with good pub food, a restaurant and the accommodation walkers want. Good base for climbing or walking (especially 5 Sisters of Kintail). A cosy refuge. LO 9pm for food.

Poosie Nansie's

Mauchline

www.mauchlinevillage.co.uk
Main street of this Ayrshire village where Burns lived in 1788. This pub was there then, those characters still there at the bar. Four of his children buried (yes, 4) in the churchyard opposite. A room in the pub left as was. Living heritage at its most apt! Lunch & 6-8pm Fri/Sat. Otherwise just the ale.

Tibbie Shiels Inn

Borders

www.tibbieshielsinn.com
Off A708 Moffat-Selkirk road. Occupies its own particular place in Scottish culture, especially literature and in the Border hills southwest of Selkirk where it nestles between two romantic lochs. On Southern Upland Way a good place to stop and refuel (very busy on Sun).

The Murray Arms & The Masonic

Gatehouse of Fleet

www.murrayarmshotel.co.uk
www.themasonic-arms.co.uk
Two adjacent unrelated pubs that fit perfectly into the life of this great wee town. The Masonic is best for food with great atmosphere. Masonic symbols still on the walls of the upstairs rooms. Murray Arms has the Burns connection. **The Ship** on the main street is the new good-lookin' kid on the block.

Lock Inn

Fort Augustus

Busy canalside (Caledonian Canal which joins Loch Ness in the distance) pub for locals and visitors. Good grub: you should book for the upstairs restaurant, The Gilliegorm. Reasonable malts. Food LO 9.30pm. Some live music. Seats on the canal in summer where boats go very frequently by.

Steampacket Inn

Isle of Whithorn
01988 500334

www.steampacketinn.com
The hub of atmospheric wee village at the end of the road south. On a harbour that fills and empties with the tide. Great for ales and food (brunch & LO 9pm all year). It is worth the long road to get here.

The selection listed here is of pubs outside Edinburgh and Glasgow: they have their own listings in Scotland the Best.

Sorn Inn

✓✓

Sorn
01290 551305

www.sorninn.com
Main street of village, 8km east of Mauchline 25 km Ayr. Pub with rooms and big reputation for food. Restaurants and tables in bar. Family-run (the Grants with chef Craig Grant). Gastropub of the Year 2005 and Michelin Bib Gourmand. Everything just so and made here, including the ice cream. Lunch & LO 9pm (8pm in bar). All day Sat/Sun.

The Inn At Kippen

✓✓

Kippen
01786 871010

www.theinnatkippen.co.uk
This is the place that put Kippen on the foodie map. Great value and excellent special menu for kids. When you add the deli and the Cross Keys (see further on in this section), Kippen is suddenly the village pub destination of central Scotland. The Inn is often fully booked. Four rooms. 7 days, lunch & LO 9pm.

The Black Bull

✓✓

Lauder
01578 722208

www.blackbull-lauder.com
Main street of ribbon town on the A68 between Edinburgh and the Borders, but near enough the city to be a destination meal. Eight individual rooms above, diverse rooms below. Some great Modern British cooking with excellent wine list. 7 days. LO 9pm.

The Summer Isles Hotel Bar

✓✓

Achiltibuie
01854 622282

www.summerisleshotel.co.uk
The adjacent bar of this longest romantic hotel on the foreshore facing the isles and the sunset. All the superior qualities of their famous (Michelin) food operation

are available at less than half the price in the cosy bistro-like bar although it is for sale at time of going to press so the standard may change in the future. Great seafood and vegetarian. Apr-Oct, lunch & LO 8.30pm.

The Grange Inn

St Andrews
01334 472670

4km out of town off Anstruther/Crail road A917. Perennially popular. Mike and Lena Singer have built on long reputation of this almost Englishy pub with cosy rooms and comfort food with flair. Lunch (not Sat) till LO 1.30pm & dinner (not Sun evening or Mon) LO 8.30pm. Must book weekends.

The Creel Inn

Catterline
Near Stonehaven
01569 750254

2km from main A92 Arbroath-Stonehaven road 8km south Stonehaven (signed) perching above the bay from where the lobsters come. And lots of other seafood. Good wine and huge speciality beer selection. Cove itself has a kind of haunting beauty. Catterline is Joan Eardley territory. Now it's also famous for this pub. 7 days lunch & LO 9pm.

The Wheatsheaf

www.wheatsheaf-swinton.co.uk

Swinton
01890 860257

A hotel pub in an undistinguished village about halfway between Kelso and Berwick (18km) on the B6461. In deepest, flattest Berwickshire, owners Chris and Jan Winson serve up the best pub grub you've had since England. Twelve rooms adjacent and in cottages. An all-round good hostelry. Lunch & 6-9.30pm.

Fox & Hounds

Houston

www.foxandhoundshouston.co.uk
On village main street in Renfrewshire, 30km west of Glasgow by M8 junction 29 (A726), then cross back under motorway on B790. Village pub and home to Houston brewery with great ales, excellent pub food and dining room upstairs for family meals and suppers. Folk come from miles around. Sunday roasts. Fine for kids. Menu from 12noon-10pm (Sun 9pm). Restaurant: 01505 612448. Bar till 12midnight.

The Cross Keys

Kippen
01786 870293

www.kippencrosskeys.co.uk
Here forever in this quiet backwater town off the A811 15km west of Stirling. With new owners '07 who want to keep it solid and the same, but make it better. We think they may succeed. Bar meals by coal fire, à la carte and family restaurants. An old-style pub-food stop, for a'body. LO 9pm.

The Wheatsheaf

Symington
01563 830307

www.wheatsymington.co.uk
2km A77. Pleasant village off the unpleasant A77 with this busy coaching inn opposite church. Folk come from miles around to eat (book at weekends) honest-to-goodness pub fare in various rooms (roast beef every Sunday). Menu on boards. Beer garden. LO 9.30pm.

Old Bridge Inn

Aviemore

www.oldbridgeinn.co.uk/aviemore
Off Coylumbridge road at south end of Aviemore as you come in from A9 or Kincraig. 100m off main street but sits in a hollow. An old inn like it says, with basic à la carte and more interesting black-board

specials. Three cask ales on tap. Kids' menu that is not just pizza and chips; ski-bums welcome. Lunch & 6-9pm. In summer, tables over road by the river. Hostel adjacent. LO 9.30pm.

Lairhillock

Near Netherley,
Stonehaven
01569 730001

www.lairhillock.co.uk
In new hands since last I ate here but known forever for great food (7 days lunch and dinner); more informal and downright friendly. Fine for kids. Superb cheese selection, and notable malts and ales. Simplest direction is: 15km south of Aberdeen by main A92 towards Stonehaven, then signed Durris, go 5km to country crossroads. The Crynoch Restaurant is adjacent.

Kilberry Inn

Near Tarbert,
Argyll
01880 770223

On the single-track B8024 that follows the coast of the Knapdale peninsula between Lochgilphead and Tarbert, this is out on its own. Fortunately Clare Johnson is a great cook (predominantly seafood) and the bar has a just-right ambience. So make the journey for lunch or dinner. LO 9pm. Closed Mon. Mar-Dec.

Kylesku Hotel

Kylesku
01971 502231

www.kyleskuhotel.co.uk
Off A894 between Scourie and Lochinver in Sutherland. A hotel and pub with a great quayside location on Loch Glencoul where boats leave for trips to see the 'highest waterfall in Europe'. Friendly atmosphere with local fish, seafood (especially with legs: the big prawn thing!) and yummy desserts. Lunch & 6-9pm Mar-Oct.

Ship Inn

Elie

www.ship-elie.com
Pub on the bay at Elie, the perfect toon in the picturesque corneresque East Neuk. In summer a huge food operation: bar, back room, next door and upstairs (latter has good view; must book weekends). Same menu throughout and blackboard specials. Real popular place especially in sunshine when terrace overlooking the beach goes like Bondi (and service can lapse). LO 9pm. Also has five rooms adjacent in summer (01333 330246).

The Ship Inn

Broughty Ferry

Excellent seafront (Tay estuary – last time we saw dolphins outside; the pub can supply binoculars) snug pub with food upstairs and down (best tables at window upstairs). Famous for its clootie dumpling. 7 days, lunch & 5-9pm.

Smiddy Bar At The Kingarth Hotel

Isle Of Bute
01700 831662

www.kingarthhotel.com
13 km Rothesay 24km after Mount Stuart. Good, friendly old inn probably serving the best food on the island. Blackboard menu. The atmosphere is just right. Open all year. Food LO 8pm.

Old Mill

Main Street,
Killearn
01360 550068

www.killearnontheweb.co.uk
There is more than one notable inn in this village but this is cosy, friendly and all an old pub should be (old here means it dates from 1774). Pub and restaurant. Log fires, nice for kids. Garden. 7 days 12noon-9pm.

Apple Inn

Troon
01292 318819

Small, unpretentious and somewhat unatmospheric pub on Irvine road out of Troon. Great eclectic menu with staples. And enough to be noticed. Lunch & LO 9.30pm (10pm weekends).

Cochrane Inn

Gateshead
01563 570122

Part of the Costley empire. A trim, ivy-covered, very inn-like inn and very agreeable. On A759 Troon to Kilmarnock and 2km A71 Kilmarnock-Irvine road. A bugger to get to (locals know how), but excellent gourmet pub with reputation. Must book weekends. Lunch & LO 9pm.

Hunting Lodge Hotel

Falkland
01337 857226

Main street of much visited town in central Fife, opposite the fabulous Palace. All-day menu of mainly stalwarts like 80/- ale steak pie and macaroni cheese. Also next door **The Covenanter Hotel** has an Italian restaurant, Luigino (01337 857224), which does a passable wood-oven pizza, pasta, etc. Both open 7 days. LO 8-9.30pm depending on the day.

Lion & Unicorn

Thornhill
01786 850204

www.lion-unicorn.co.uk
On A873 off A84 between M9 and Callander; near Lake of Menteith in the Trossachs. On main road through nondescript village. They come from miles around for pub grub and sizzling steaks. Cosy dining areas; garden. Changing menu, not fancy. 7 days. LO 9pm.

Badachro Inn

Badachro
Near Gairloch
01445 741255

South of Gairloch off A832, then B8056 to Redpoint. A spectacular road and fantastic setting for this waterside pub. Great beer and wine list with lots by the glass and great home-made pub grub.

Probably tickworthy but le patron comes with a bit of attitude that some visitors could do without (not of course, regular Jamiroquai, who lives nearby). 7 days 12noon-3pm, 6-9pm.

Goblin Ha' Hotel

Gifford
01620 810244

www.goblinha.com
Twee village in East Lothian heartland. This hotel with the great name serves a decent pub lunch and supper (6-9pm; 9.30pm on Fri and Sat) in lounge and more basic version in the pub. Conservatory and 'Biergarten'; kids' play area. Recent chain takeover with more pasta/pizza and less panache.

The Byre

Brig o' Turk
01877 376292

Off A821 at Callander end of the village by Dundarroch Hotel and Loch Achray. Country inn in deepest Trossachs. Less gastro, more basic pub grub in cosy rooms with outside deck in summer. You can walk from here to Duke's Pass.

The Crown

Portpatrick
01776 810261

Hugely popular pub on the harbour with tables outside in summer. Light, airy conservatory at back serving freshly caught fish. 12 rooms above. Locals and Irish who sail over for lunch (sic). LO 10pm.

Auld Cross Keys Inn

Denholm
Near Hawick
01450 870305

Not a lot to recommend in Hawick, so this village pub with rooms is worth the 8km journey on the A698 Jedburgh road. On the Green, with pub and dining lounges through the back. Blackboard menu, heaps of choice. Curries on Mon/Tue. Real fire and candles. Sun carvery. Food LO 8pm. Three rooms if you want to stay.

Part 3

Scot
land
the
best

Some Of
The Best
Places
To Visit

☕ – *signifies notable tearoom.*

Free / Admission – indicates entry fee due – or not.
NTS – garden under the care of the National Trust for Scotland.

The Younger Botanic Garden

✓✓
Benmore

www.rbge.org.uk
12km Dunoon on the A815 to Strachur. An 'outstation' of the Royal Botanic in Edinburgh, gifted to the nation in 1928, but the first plantations dating from 1820. Walks marked through formal gardens, woody grounds and the 'pinetum' where the air is often so sweet and spicy it can seem like the elixir of life. Redwood avenue, terraced hills, views; a garden of different moods and fine proportions. Café. Apr-Sep 10am-6pm (5pm Oct-Mar).

Inverewe

✓✓
Poolewe
Admission
NTS
☕

www.nts.org.uk
On A832, 80km south of Ullapool. World-famous gardens on a promontory of Loch Ewe. Helped by the ameliorating effect of the Gulf Stream, the 'wild' garden became the model for many others. The guided tours (1.30pm Mon-Fri Apr-Sep) are probably the best way to get the most out of this extensive garden. Gardens all year till dusk – go in the evening when it's quiet! Shop, visitor centre till 5pm.

Crathes

✓✓
Near Banchory
Admission
NTS
☕

www.nts.org.uk
25km west of Aberdeen and just off A93 on Royal Deeside. Interesting tower house surrounded by mind-blowing topiary and walled gardens of inspired design and tranquil atmosphere. Keen gardeners will be in a scented heaven. The Golden Garden (after Gertrude Jekyll) works particularly well and there's a wild garden beyond the old wall that

many miss. All in all, a very *House and Garden* experience though in summer it's stuffed with people as well as plants. Grounds open all year 9am-sunset.

Little Sparta

Near Dunsyre
01899 810252
Admission

www.littlesparta.org
Near Biggar southwest of Edinburgh off A702 (5km), go through village then signed. House in bare hill country the home of conceptual artist and national treasure, Ian Hamilton Finlay who died in 2006. Gardens lovingly created over years, full of thought-provoking art/sculpture/perspectives. Unlike anywhere else. A privilege to visit. Jun-Sep, Fri & Sun 2-5pm only.

Drummond Castle Gardens

Muthill
Admission

www.drummongcastlegardens.co.uk
Near Crieff; signed from A822, 2km from Muthill then up a long avenue, the most exquisite formal gardens viewed first from the terrace by the house. A box-wood parterre of a vast St Andrew's Cross in yellow and red (especially antirrhinums and roses), the Drummond colours, with extraordinary sundial centrepiece; five gardeners keep every leaf in place. 7 days Easter & May-Oct 1-5pm (last admission). House not open to public.

Logan Botanical Gardens

✓✓

Near Sandhead

www.rbge.org.uk
16km south of Stranraer by A77/A716 and 2km on from Sandhead. Compact and full of pleasant southern surprises. Less crowded than other 'exotic' gardens. Their 'soundwands' giving commentary on demand make it all very interesting. Coffee shop decent. The Gunnera Bog is quite extraterrestrial. Mar-Oct; 7 days, 10am-5pm (6pm Apr-Sep).

Crarae

Inveraray
NTS

www.nts.org.uk
16km southeast on A83 to Lochgilphead.
Famed and fabulous. Recently taken over
by NTS so difficulties in staying open
resolved. The wooded banks of Loch Fyne
with gushing burn are as lush as the
jungles of Borneo. All year 10am till dusk.
Visitor centre till 5pm.

Dunrobin Castle Gardens

Golspie
Admission

On A9 1km north of town. Versailles-
inspired gardens sit below the opulent
Highland chateau of the Dukes of
Sutherland. Terraced, parterred and im-
maculate, they stretch to the sea. Thirty
gardeners once tended them; now there
are four but little has changed. Apr-Oct
10.30am-last admission 4pm (5pm Jun-
Sep).

Glenwhan

Near Glen Luce,
Near Solway
Coast
Admission

Signed from A75 and close to more
famous Castle Kennedy (also very much
worth a visit), this the more edifying
labour of love. Up through beechy (and in
May) bluebell woods and through back-
yards to horticultural haven teased from
moorland in 1979. Open moorland still
beckons at the top of the network of trails
through a carefully planted botanical
wonder. Many seats, some sculpture.
Easter-Sep 10am-5pm.

Threave

Near Castle
Douglas
Admission

64 acres of magnificent Victorian
landscaping in an incomparable setting
overlooking the Galloway coastline.
Gardeners shouldn't miss the walled
kitchen garden. Horticulturally inspiring;
and also daunting. Open Feb-Dec 10am-
dusk.

Dawyck

Stobo
Admission

www.rbge.org.uk
On B712 Moffat road off A72 Biggar/
Peebles road, 2km from Stobo. Another
Edinburgh Botanics outstation; a 'recent'
acquisition, though tree planting here
goes back 300 years. Sloping grounds
around the gurgling Scrape burn which
trickles into the Tweed. Landscaped
woody pathways for meditative walks.
Famous for shrubs, blue Himalayan pop-
pies and 'the azalea terrace'. Great walk
on Drovers road, 2km off Stobo Rd before
entrance. Tiny tearoom being developed.
Mar-Oct 10am-5pm.

Angus' Garden

Taynuilt
Honesty Box

www.barguillean.co.uk
7km from village (which is 12km from
Oban on the A85) on Glen Lonan road.
Take first right after Barguillen Garden
Centre. A garden laid out by the family
who own the centre in memory of their
son Angus, a soldier, who was killed in
Cyprus. On the slopes by a small loch
brimful of lilies and ducks. Informal mix
of tended and uncultivated (though wild
prevails), a more poignant remembrance
is hard to imagine as you while an hour
away in this peaceful place. Open all year.

Dr Neil's (Secret) Garden

Edinburgh
Honesty Box

At least a few people know about this
superb, almost private garden on the
shores of Duddingston Loch. At the end
of the road through Holyrood Park, just
past Duddingston church, enter through
the manse gates. Turn right. At end of the
manse lawn, in the corner a gate leads to
an extraordinary terraced garden border-
ing the loch. With wild Arthur's Seat
above, you'd swear you were in Argyll.
The labour of love of one Claudia Poitier

and many volunteers, this is an enchanting corner of the city. 7 days dawn-dusk. The skating minister (Raeburn) was here.

Arduaine Garden

✓

Near Kilmelford
NTS
Admission

www.arduaine-garden.org.uk

28km south of Oban on A816, one of Argyll's undiscovered arcadias gifted to the NTS and brought to wider attention. Creation of the microclimate in which the rich, diverse vegetation has flourished, influenced by Osgood Mackenzie of Inverewe and its restoration a testimony to 20 years' hard labour by the Wright brothers. Enter/park by Loch Melfort hotel, gate 100m. Until dusk.

Achamore Garden

✓

Isle of Gigha
Admission

www.gigha.org.uk

1km from ferry. Walk or cycle (bike hire at post office at top of ferry road); an easy day trip. The 'big house' (which does great B&B) on the island set in 65 acres. Lush tropical plants mingle with early-flourishing rhodies (Feb-March): all due to the mild climate and the devotion of only two gardeners. Two marked walks (40 minutes/2 hours) start from the walled garden (green route takes in the sea view of Islay and Jura). Density and variety of shrubs, pond plants and trees revealed as you meander. Leaflet guides. Open all year dawn to dusk.

Drum Castle Rose Garden

✓

Near Banchory
NTS

www.nts.org.uk

1km from A93, the Deeside road. In the grounds of Drum Castle (the Irvine ancestral home), a superb walled garden paying homage to the rose and encapsulating four centuries of its horticulture. Four areas (from 17th to 20th centuries). Fabulous, Jul/Aug especially. 10am-6pm.

Ascog Hall Fernery

Rothesay
Admission

www.ascoghallfernery.co.uk
Outside town on road to Mount Stuart, it's worth stopping at this small garden and very small Victorian Fern House. Green and lush and dripping! Easter-Oct, 10am-5pm. Closed Mon/Tue. (And don't miss Rothesay's Victorian men's loos (women can visit); they are not small.

Priorwood

Melrose
NTS
Admission

www.nts.org.uk
Next to Melrose Abbey, a tranquil secret garden behind high walls specialises in growing flowers and plants for drying. Picking, drying and arranging is continuously in progress. Samples for sale. Also includes a historical apple orchard with trees through the ages. Sadly the heavenly jelly is no longer on sale (damn 'Health 'n' Safety'). Mon-Sat 10am-5pm; Sun 1.30-5pm. Closed 4pm winter.

Kailzie Gardens

Peebles
Admission

www.kailziegardens.com
On B7062 Traquair road. Informal woodland gardens just out of town; not extensive but eminently strollable. Old-fashioned roses and wilder bits. Some poor birds in cages and the odd peacock. Courtyard teashop. Kids' corner. Fishing pond popular. Apr-Oct 11am-5.30pm (restricted access in winter).

Monteviot House Garden & Woodside Nursery

Near Ancrum
and Jedburgh
Admission

Off A68 at Ancrum, the B6400 to Nisbet (3km), first there's Woodside on left (the Victorian walled garden for the house – now separate) and the terraced-to-the-river (Teviot), mainly formal gardens of the house (the home of the Tory Nicholas

Soames, now Lord Lothian). Very pleasant to amble. Woodside has organic demonstrations section and is mainly a garden centre. House: 2 weeks in Jul 1-5pm. Gardens: Apr-Oct 12noon-5pm. Nursery: Mar-Oct 9.30am-5.30pm.

Pitmedden Garden

Near Ellon
NTS
Admission
☕

www.nts.org.uk

35km north of Aberdeen, 10km west of A92. Formal French gardens recreated in 1950s on site of Sir Alex Seaton's 17th-century ones. The four great parterres, three based on designs for Holyrood Palace gardens, are best viewed from the terrace. Charming farmhouse 'museum' seems transplanted. For lovers of symmetry and an orderly universe only (but there is a woodland walk with wildlife garden area). May-Sep 10am-5.30pm.

Pitoddrie House

Chapel of
Garioch
Near Inverurie

www.macdonaldhotels.co.uk

An exceptional walled garden in the grounds of Pittodrie House Hotel in Aberdeenshire. Different gardens compartmentalised by hedges. 500m from house and unvisited by most of the guests, this secret and sheltered haven is both a kitchen garden and a place for meditations and reflections (and possibly wedding photos).

Ardkinglas Woodland

Cairndow
Honesty Box

www.ardkinglass.com

Off the A83 Loch Lomond to Inveraray road. Through village to signed car park and these mature woodlands in the grounds of Ardkinglas House on the southern bank near the head of Loch Fyne. Fine pines include the 'tallest tree in Britain'. Magical at dawn or dusk.

Jura House Walled Garden

Ardfin, Jura
Admission

www.jurahouseandgardens.co.uk
8km from the ferry. Park opposite, follow track into woods. Walled garden only part of walk that takes you to coast and ultimately (though steep) to the beach and the 'Misty Pools'. Beautiful in rain (frequent) or shine! Open all year 9am-5pm.

Attadale Gardens

Strathcarron
Admission

www.attadale.com
On A890 from Kyle of Lochalsh and A87 south of Strathcarron. Lovely Highland house and gardens near Loch Carron. Exotic specials, water gardens, sculpture, great rhodies May/Jun. Nursery and kitchen garden. New fern garden and Japanese garden '07. Good restaurant nearby. Apr-Oct 10am-5pm. Closed Sun.

The Hydroponicum

Achildtibuie
01854 622202
Admission

www.thehydroponicum.com
The 'Garden of the Future': an indoor water world where plants thrive without soil in their own microclimates. Apr-Sep (and Oct weekends). Tours hourly. Growing kits to buy (strawberries at Christmas?). Café, exhibition 11am-4pm.

Ard-Daraich Hill Garden

Ardgour
01855 841348

www.ard-daraich.co.uk
3 km south Ardgour at Corran Ferry on A861 to Strontian. Private, labour of love 'hill' and wild garden where you are free to wander. Specialises in rhodies, shrubs, trees. Nursery/small garden centre. Open all year, 7 days.

The Hidden Gardens

Glasgow

www.thehiddengardens.org.uk
A garden oasis and a sanctuary in the city behind the Tramway. Open 10am-8pm (winter hours vary). Closed Mon.

Plockton

Near Kyle of Lochalsh

www.plockton.com
A Highland gem of a place 8km over the hill from Kyle, clustered around inlets of a wooded bay on Loch Carron. Cottage gardens down to the bay and palm trees! Some great walks over headlands. Plockton Inn probably best bet for reasonable stay and eats. Plockton Hotel and the new excellent Plockton Shores. It's not hard to feel connected with this village (and so many people do).

Moray Coast Fishing Villages

From Spey Bay to Fraserburgh

Some of Scotland's best coastal scenery and many interesting villages in cliff/cove and beach settings. Especially notable are **Portsoy** with 17th-century harbour; **Sandend** with its own popular beach and a fabulous one nearby; **Pennan** made famous by the film *Local Hero* and its recent mudslide; **Gardenstown** (has a great café/restaurant at the harbour) with a walk along the water's edge to **Crovie** (pronounced 'Crivee'), the epitome of a coast-clinging community; and **Cullen**, which is more of a town and has a great beach.

Stromness

Orkney Mainland

24km from Kirkwall and a different kettle of fish. Hugging the shore and with narrow streets and wynds, it has a unique atmosphere that's both maritime and European. Some of the most singular shops you'll see anywhere and the Orkney folk going about their business. Park near harbour and walk down the cobbled main street if you don't want to scrape your paintwork.

Cromarty

Near Inverness

At end of road across Black Isle from Inverness (45km northeast). Village with dreamy, times-gone-by atmosphere without being twee. Lots of kids running about and a pink strand of beach. Delights to discover include: the east kirk, plain and ascetic with countryside through the windows behind the altar; Hugh (the geologist) Miller's cottage/Courthouse museum; The Pantry; Cromarty Bakery; the perfect, wee restaurant Sutor Creek; the shore and cliff walk; the Pirates' Cemetery; and of course the dolphins.

Culross

Near Dunfermline

By A994 from Dunfermline or junction 1 of M90. Old centre conserved and being restored by NTS. Mainly residential and not awash with craft and coffee shops. More historical than merely quaint; a community of careful custodians lives in the white and yellow red-pantiled houses. Footsteps echo in the cobbled wynds. Palace and Town House open Easter-Oct 10am-6pm, weekends only Oct. Interesting back gardens and lovely church at top of hill. Pamphlet by Rights of Way Society available locally, is useful.

Tobermory

Mull

Not so much a village or setting for the yesteryear *Balamory*, rather the main town of Mull, set around a hill on superb bay. Ferry port for Ardnamurchan, but main Oban ferry is 35km away at Craignure. Usually a bustling harbour front with quieter streets behind; a quintessential island atmosphere. Some good inexpensive hotels (and quayside hostel) well situated to explore the whole island.

Port Charlotte

Islay

A township on the 'Rhinns of Islay', the western peninsula. By A846 from the ports, Askaig and Ellen via Bridgend. Rows of whitewashed, well-kept cottages along and back from shoreline. On the road in there's an island museum and a coffee/bookshop. Also a 'town' beach and one between Port Charlotte and Bruichladdich (and especially the one with the war memorial nearby). Quiet and charming, not merely quaint.

Rockcliffe

Near Dumfries

25km south on Solway Coast road, A710. On the 'Scottish Riviera', the rocky part of the coast around to Kippford. A good rock-scrambling foreshore though not so clean, and a village with few houses and Baron's Craig hotel; set back with great views but a somewhat gloomy presence. Tearoom in village.

East Neuk Villages

Around the Firth of Forth, Fife

www.eastneukwide.co.uk
Quintessential quaint wee fishing villages. **Crail, Anstruther, Pittenweem, St Monans** and **Elie** all have different characters and attractions especially Crail and Pittenweem harbours; Anstruther as main centre and home of Fisheries Museum; and perfect Elie. Best to see by cycling. Summer traffic not good.

Aberdour

Between Dunfermline and Kirkcaldy

www.aberdour.org.uk
Near Forth Road Bridge (10km east from junction 1 of M90) or, better still, go by train from Edinburgh (frequent service); delightful station. Walks round harbour and to headland, Silver Sands beach 1km, castle ruins.

Diabeg

Between Dunfermline and Kirkcaldy

On north shore of Loch Torridon at the end of the unclassified road from Torridon on one of Scotland's most inaccessible peninsulas. Diabeg is simply beautiful (though pity about those fish cages). Fantastic road there and then walk! PS: there's no pub, though a local wifie may do you tea and buns in season – ask around!

Isle of Whithorn

South West

www.isleofwhithorn.com
Strange faraway village at end of the road, 35km south Newton Stewart, 6km Whithorn. Mystical harbour where low tide does mean low, a saintly shoreline, a sea angler's pub, **The Steam Packet** – very good pub grub. Great deli/pizzeria – **Ravenstones**. Ninian's chapel round the headland not so uplifting but en route you'll see the *Solway Harvester* memorial by the white building. Everybody visiting Whithorn seems to walk this way.

Corrie

Arran

www.arran.uk.com
Last but not least, the bonniest bit of Arran (apart from Kildonan and the glens, etc), best reached by bike from Brodick (01770 302244 or 302868). Many walks from here including Goat Fell but nice just to sit or potter on the foreshore. Hotel has never lived up to expectations but the village shop is fab. I'd like a memorial bench on this very shoreline.

Pete's Beach

Near Durness

The One of many great beaches on the North Coast that I've called my own. The hill above it is called 'Ceannabeinne'; you find it 7km east of Durness. Coming from Tongue it's just after where Loch Eriboll comes out to the sea and the road hits the coast again (there's a layby opposite). It's a small perfect cove flanked by walls of coral-pink rock and shallow turquoise sea. Splendid from above (land rises to a bluff with a huge boulder) and from below. There's a bench – come sit by me then leave your footprints in the sand.

Kiloran Beach

Colonsay

9km from quay and hotel, past Colonsay House: parking and access on hill side. Often described as the finest beach in the Hebrides, it does not disappoint though it has changed character in recent years (a shallower sandbar traps tidal run-off). Craggy cliffs on one side, negotiable rocks on the other and, in between, tiers of grassy dunes. Do go to the end! Colonsay was once bought as a picnic spot. This beach was probably the reason why.

Moray Coast

From Spey Bay to Fraserburgh

www.moray.gov.uk
Many great beaches along this coast, notably **Cullen** and **Lossiemouth** (town beaches); **New Aberdour** (1km from village on B9031) and **Rosehearty** (8km west of Fraserburgh) both quieter places for walks and picnics. One of the best-kept secrets is the beach at **Sunnyside** where you walk past the incredible ruins of Findlater Castle on the cliff top (how did they build it? A place, on its grassed-over roof, for a picnic) and down to a cove which on my sunny day was just perfect.

Macrihanish

Kintyre Peninsula

At the bottom of the Kintyre peninsula 10km from Campbeltown. Walk north from Machrihanish village or golf course, or from the car park on the main A83 to Tayinloan and Tarbert at point where it hits/leaves the coast. A joyously long strand (8km) of unspoiled orange-pink sand backed by dunes and facing the 'steepe Atlantic Stream' all the way to Newfoundland.

Sandwood Bay

Near Kinlochbervie

This mile-long sandy strand with its old 'Stack', is legendary, but therein lies the problem since now too many people know about it and you may have to share its glorious isolation. Inaccessibility is its saving grace: a 7km walk from the sign off the road at Balchrick (near the cattle grid), 6km from Kinlochbervie or cut a third of the distance in a 4-wheel drive; allow 3 hours return plus time there. Go easy and go in summer! Also:

Oldshoremore

Near Kinlochbervie

The beach you pass on the road to Balchrick, only 3km from Kinlochbervie. It's easy to reach and a beautiful spot: the water is clear and perfect for swimming, and there are rocky walks and quiet places. Polin, 500m north, is a cove you might have to yourself.

Saligo, Machir Bay & The Big Strand

Islay

www.islayinfo.com

The first two are bays on northwest of island via A847 road to Port Charlotte, then B8018 past Loch Gorm. Wide beaches; remains of war fortifications in deep dunes, Machir perhaps best for beach bums. They say 'no swimming' so

paddle with extreme prejudice. The Big
Strand on Laggan Bay: along Bowmore-
Port Ellen road take Oa turnoff, follow
Kintra signs. There's camping and great
walks in either direction, 8km of glorious
sand and dunes (with the Machrie Golf
Course). An airy amble under a wide sky.

Ostal Beach/Kilbride Bay

✓

*Millhouse near
Tighnabruaich*

3km from Millhouse on B8000 signed
Ardlamont (not Portvadie, the ferry), a
track to right before white house (often
with a chain across to restrict access).
Park and walk 1.5km, turning right after
lochan. You arrive on a perfect white
sandy crescent known locally as Ostal
and, apart from the odd swatch of
sewage, in certain conditions a mystical
secret place to swim and picnic. The
north coast of Arran is like a Greek island
in the bay.

South Uist

✓

Outer Hebrides

www.southuist.com
Deserted but for birds, an almost
unbroken strand of beach running for
miles down the west coast; the machair
at its best early summer. Take any road
off the spinal A865; usually less than
2km. Good spot to try is turnoff at Tobha
Mor; real blackhouses and a chapel on
the way to the sea.

Scarista Beach

✓

South Harris

On main road south of Tarbert (15km) to
Rodel. The beach is so beautiful that people have been married there. Hotel over
the road is worth staying just for this, but
is also a great retreat – also two excellent
self-catering cottages. Golf course on
links. Fab in early evening. The sun also
rises.

Lunan Bay

Near Montrose

5km from main A92 road to Aberdeen and 5km of deep red crescent beach under a wide northern sky. But 'n' Ben, Auchmithie, is an excellent place to start or finish and good approach (from south), although Gordon's restaurant at Inverkeilor is closer. Best viewpoint from Boddin Farm 3km south Montrose and 3km from A92 signed 'Usan'. Often deserted.

The Secret Beach

Near Achmelvich

Approach from Achmelvich car park going north (it's the next proper bay round) or Lochinver-Stoer/Drumbeg road: less walk, layby on right 3km after Achmelvich turnoff, 250m beyond sign for 'Cathair Estate'. Park on right (going north) and walk towards sea on left following stream (a sign points to 'Mill'). Well-defined path. Called Alltan na Bradhan, it's the site of an old mill (grinding wheels still there), perfect for camping and the best sea for swimming in the area. A tiny patch of sand to call your own.

Lowlandman's Bay

Jura

www.theisleofjura.co.uk
Not strictly a beach (there is a sandy strand before the headland) but a rocky foreshore with ethereal atmosphere; great light and space. Only seals break the spell. Go right at the three-arch bridge to first group of houses (Knockdrome), through yard on left and right around cottages to track to Ardmenish. After deer fences, bay is visible on your right, 1km walk away.

Vatersay

Outer Hebrides

The tiny island joined by a causeway to Barra. Twin crescent beaches on either side of the isthmus, one shallow and sheltered visible from Castlebay, the other an ocean beach with rollers. Dunes/machair; safe swimming. There's a helluva hill between Barra and Vatersay if you're cycling.

Seal Bay

Barra

www.isleofbarra.com

5km Castlebay on west coast, 2km after Isle of Barra Hotel through gate across machair where road right is signed Taobh a Deas Allathasdal. A flat, rocky Hebridean shore and skerries where seals flop into the water and eye you with intense curiosity. The better-beach beach is next to the hotel.

West Sands

St Andrews

As a town beach, this is hard to beat; it dominates the view to west. Wide swathe not too unclean and sea swimmable. Golf courses behind. Consistently gets 'the blue flag', but beach buffs may prefer Kinshaldy or Kingsbarns (10km south on Crail road), or Elie (28km south) where there is a great beach walk taking in the Cammo Estate (and gardens) and skirting the great Kingsbarns Golf Course.

North Coast

West of Thurso

Some of Britain's most unspoiled and unsung beaches. No beach bums, no Beach Boys. There are so many great little coves, you can have one to yourself even on a hot day, but those to mention are: **Strathy** and **Armadale** (35km west Thurso), **Farr** and **Torrisdale** (48km) and **Coldbackie** (65km). My favourite is elevated to the top of this category.

Sands of Morar

Near Mallaig

70km west of Fort William and 6km from Mallaig by newly improved road, these easily accessible beaches may seem overpopulated on summer days and the south stretch nearest to Arisaig may have one too many caravan parks, but they go on for miles and there's enough space for everybody. The sand's supposed to be silver but in fact it's a very pleasing pink. Lots of rocky bits for exploration. One of the best beachy bits (the bay before the estuary) is 'Camusdarrach', signed from the main road (where *Local Hero* was filmed); further off road, it is quieter and a very good swathe of sand. Traigh, the golf course makes good use of the dunes.

The Bay at the Back of the Ocean

Iona

Easy 2km walk from frequent ferry from Fionnphort, south of Mull or hire a bike from the store on your left as you walk into the village (01681 700357). Paved road most of way. Former Labour leader John Smith, who is buried beside the abbey, once told me that this was one of his favourite places. There are two great inexpensive hotels on Iona, The Argyll and St Columba.

Dornoch (& Embo) Beaches

Dornoch Firth

The wide and extensive sandy beach of this pleasant town at the mouth of the Dornoch Firth famous also for its golf links. 4km north, Embo Sands starts with ghastly caravan city, but walk north towards Golspie. Embo is twinned with Kaunakakai, Hawaii!

Port of Ness

Isle of Lewis

Also signed Port Nis, this is the beach at the end of the Hebrides in the far north of Lewis. Just keep driving. There are some interesting art gallery and museum stops on the way – until you get to this tiny bay and harbour down the hill at the end of the road. Anthony Barber's Harbour View Gallery full of his own work (which you find in many other galleries and even postcards) is worth a visit (10am-5pm, closed Sun).

Two Beaches in the far South West

Killantringan Bay
Near Portpatrick

Off A77 before Portpatrick signed 'Dunskey Gardens' in summer, follow road signed **Killantringan** Lighthouse (dirt track). Park 1km before lighthouse. Beautiful bay for exploration. **Sandhead Beach** A716 south of Stranraer. Shallow, safe waters of Luce Bay. Perfect for families (in their damned caravans).

Robert Burns (1759–96)

Alloway, Ayr and Dumfries

www.robertburns.org

A well-marked heritage trail through his life and haunts in Ayrshire and Dumfriesshire. His howff at Dumfries is very atmospheric.

Best is at **Alloway**. The Auld Brig o' Doon and the Auld Kirk, where Tam o' Shanter saw the witches dance are all evocative, and the monument and surrounding gardens are lovely. 1km up the road, the cottage, his birthplace, has little atmosphere (now NTS at last, improvements afoot but afar). The Tam o' Shanter Experience visitor centre gets mobbed but could not be recommended.

Ayr The Auld Kirk off main street by river; graveyard with diagram of where his friends are buried; open at all times.

Dumfries House where he spent his last years and mausoleum 250m away at back of a kirkyard stuffed with extravagant masonry.

10km north of Dumfries on A76 at **Ellisland Farm** (home 1788–91) is the most interesting of all the sites. The farmhouse with genuine memorabilia, eg his mirror, fishing-rod, a poem scratched on glass, original manuscripts. There's his favourite walk by the river where he composed *Tam o' Shanter* and a strong atmosphere about the place. Open 7 days summer, closed Sun/Mon in winter.

Brow Well near Ruthwell on the B725 20km south of Dumfries and near Caerlaverock, is a quiet place, a well with curative properties where he went in the latter stages of his illness. Not many folk go to this one.

Burns and a' That Festival in May: once great. Being rethought as we speak.

Lewis Grassic Gibbon (1901-35)

Arbuthnott
Near Stonehaven

www.grassicgibbon.com

Although James Leslie Mitchell left the area in 1917, this is where he was born and spent his formative years. Visitor Centre (01561 361668; Apr-Oct 7 days 10am-4.30pm) at the end of the village (via B967, 16km south of Stonehaven off main A92) has details of his life and can point you in the direction of the places he writes about in his trilogy, *A Scots Quair*.

The first part, *Sunset Song*, is generally considered to be one of the great Scots novels and this area, the **Howe of the Mearns**, is the place he so effectively evokes.

Arbuthnott is reminiscent of 'Kinraddie' and the churchyard 1km away on the other side of road still has the atmosphere of that time of innocence before the war which pervades the book. His ashes are here in a grave in a corner; the inscription: 'the kindness of friends/the warmth of toil/the peace of rest'. From 1928 to when he died 7 years later at the age of only 34, he wrote an incredible 17 books.

Neil Gunn (1891-1973)

Dunbeath
Near Wick

www.neilgunn.org.uk

Scotland's foremost writer on Highland life, only recently receiving the recognition he deserves, was brought up in this North East fishing village and based three of his greatest yarns here, particularly *Highland River*, which must stand in any literature as a brilliant evocation of place. The **Strath** in which it is set is below the house (a nondescript terraced house next to the Stores) and makes for a great walk. There's a commemorative statue by the

the harbour, not quite the harbour you imagine from the books. The excellent heritage centre depicts the Strath on its floor and has a leaflet for you to follow.

Gunn also lived for many years near **Dingwall** and there is a memorial on the back road to Strathpeffer and a wonderful view in a place he often walked (on A834, 4km from Dingwall).

James Hogg (1770-1835)

St Mary's Loch, Ettrick

'The Ettrick Shepherd' who wrote one of the great works of Scottish literature, *Confessions of a Justified Sinner*, was born, lived and died in the valleys of the **Yarrow** and the **Ettrick**, some of the most starkly beautiful landscapes in Scotland. **St Mary's Loch** on the A708, 28km west of Selkirk: there's a commemorative statue looking over the loch and the adjacent and supernatural seeming Loch of the Lowes.

On the strip of land between is **Tibbie Shiels** pub (and hotel), once a gathering place for the writer and his friends (e.g. Sir Walter Scott) and still a notable hostelry. Across the valley divide 11km on foot, part of the Southern Upland Way, or 25km by road past the Gordon Inn, Yarrow, is the remote village of **Ettrick**, another monument and his grave (and Tibbie Shiels') in the churchyard. His countryside is stark and beautiful.

The James Hogg exhibition is at Bowhill House Visitor Centre (01750 22204).

Sir Walter Scott (1771-1832)

Abbotsford, Melrose

No other place in Scotland (and few anywhere) contains so much of a writer's life and work. This was the house he rebuilt from the farmhouse he moved to in 1812 in the countryside he did so much to popularise. The house, until recently lived in by his descendants, is run by trustees. The library and study are pretty much as he left them, with 9,000 rare books, antiquarian even in his day. Pleasant grounds and topiary and a walk by the Tweed which the house overlooks.

His grave is at **Dryburgh Abbey**. House open daily 9.30am-5pm; Sun 2-5pm (in winter 10am).

Robert Louis Stevenson (1850-94)

Edinburgh

Though Stevenson travelled widely he spent the first 30 years of his short life in Edinburgh. He was born and brought up in the New Town, living at **17 Heriot Row** from 1857 to 1880 in a fashionable town house which is still lived in (not open to the public). This area was bounded then by parkland and farms. Both the **Botanics** and **Warriston Cemetery** are part of the landscape of his childhood.

However, his fondest recollections were of the **Pentland Hills** and, unchanged as they are, it's here that one is following most poignantly in his footsteps. The 'cottage' at **Swanston** (a delightful village with some remarkable thatched cottages reached via the city bypass/ Colinton turnoff or from Oxgangs Rd and a bridge over the bypass; the village nestles in a grove of trees below the hills and is a good place to walk from), the ruins of **Glencorse Church** (ruins even then and where he later asked that a prayer be said for him) and **Colinton Manse** can all be seen, but not visited.

Edinburgh has no Stevenson Museum, but **The Writers' Museum** at Makars' Court has exhibits (of other writers also). The **Hawes Inn** in South Queensferry where he wrote *Kidnapped* has had its history obliterated by a brewery makeover.

J.K. Rowling

*Edinburgh
and elsewhere*

www.jkrowling.com

Scotland's most successful writer ever as the creator of Harry Potter, rich beyond her wildest dreams, was once (and famously) an impecunious single mother scribbling away in Edinburgh coffee shops. The most-mentioned is opposite the Festival Theatre and is now a Chinese restaurant (upstairs), but not listed. The **Elephant House** was another and gives you the idea. Harry Potter country as interpreted by Hollywood can be found at **Glenfinnan** and **Glencoe** especially around the **Clachaig Inn**.

JKR lives near Aberfeldy – you might see her in another coffee shop, the one at the **House of Menzies**, though she no longer scribbles publicly.

Irvine Welsh (b.1958)

Edinburgh

www.irvinewelsh.net

Literary immortality awaits confirmation. Tours (*that* toilet etc) likely any day. **Robbie's Bar** on Leith Walk might suffice; you will hear the voices.

*There are almost 300 hills in Scotland over 3,000ft as tabled by
Sir Hugh Munro in 1891. Those selected have been chosen for
their relative ease of access both to the bottom and thence the
top. All offer rewarding climbs. None should be attempted
without proper clothing (especially boots) and sustenance. You
may also need an OS map. Never underestimate how quickly
weather conditions can change in the Scottish mountains.*

Ben Lomond

*Rowardennan,
Loch Lomond*

Many folk's first Munro, given proximity
to Glasgow (soul and city). It's not too
taxing a climb and has rewarding views
(in good weather). Two main ascents:
'tourist route' is easier, from toilet block
at Rowardennan car park (end of road
from Drymen), well-trodden all the way;
or 500m up past Youth Hostel, a path follows burn – the 'Ptarmigan Route'.
Steeper, but quieter. Circular walk possible. 974m. 3 hours up.

Schiehallion

*Near
Kinloch Rannoch*

'Fairy Hill of the Caledonians' and a bit of
a must. New path c/o John Muir Trust
over east flank. Start Braes of Foss car
park 10k from Kinloch Rannoch. 10km
walk, ascent 750m. 6 hours. 1,083m.

Carn Aosda

Glenshee

One of the most accessible. Starting from
Glenshee ski car park follow ski tow up.
Ascent only 270m of 917m. So you can
bag a Munro in an hour. Easier still, take
chairlift to Cairnwell, take in peak behind
and then Carn Aosda – hey, you're doing
three Munros in a morning. The
Grampian Highlands unfold.

Meall Chuaich

Dalwhinnie

Starting from verge of the A9 south of
Cuaich ascent only 623m, total walk
14km. Follow aqueduct to power station
then Loch Cuaich. An easily bagged 951m.

An Teallach

Torridon

Sea-level start from Dundonnell on the A832 south of Ullapool. One of the most awesome Scots peaks but not the ordeal it looks. Path well trod; great scrambling opportunities. Peering over the pinnacle of Lord Berkeley's Seat into the void is a jaw-drop. Take a day. Nice coffee shop called Maggie's near start/finish. 1,062m.

Beinn Alligin

Torridon

The other great Torridon trek. Consult re start at Torridon visitor centre on road. Car park by bridge on road to Inveralligin and Diabeg, walk through woods over moor by river. Steepish pull up onto the Horns of Alligin. You can cover two Munros in a circular route that takes you across the top of the world. 985m.

Ben More

Mull

The 'cool, high ben' sits in isolated splendour, the only Munro, bar the Cuillins, not on the mainland. Sea-level start from layby on the coast road B8073 that skirts the southern coast of Loch Na Keal at Dhiseig House, then a fairly clear path through the bleak landscape. Tricky near the top but there are fabulous views across the islands. 966m.

Ben Wyvis

Near Garve

Standing apart from its northern neighbours, you can feel the presence of this mountain from a long way off. North of main A835 road Inverness-Ullapool and very accessible from it, park 6km north of Garve (48km from Inverness) and follow marked path by stream through the shattered remnants of what was once a forest (replanting in progress). Leave the dereliction behind; the summit approach is by a soft, mossy ridge. Magnificent 1,046m.

Lochnagar

Near Ballater

Lochnagar's nobility and mystique apparent from afar, not least Balmoral. Approach via Glen Muick (pron. 'Mick') road from Ballater to Loch Muick car park. Path to mountain well signed. 18km return, allow 6-8 hours. Steep at top; the loch supernatural. Apparently on a clear day you can see the Forth Bridge. 1,155m.

Bla Bheinn

Skye

This magnificent massif (pronounced 'Blahven') has a sea-level start and seems higher than it is. The *Munro Guide* says it is 'exceptionally accessible'. It has an eerie jagged beauty and, though some scrambling is involved and it helps to have a head for exposed situations, there are no serious dangers. Take B8083 from Broadford to Elgol through Torrin, park 1km south of the head of Loch Slapin, walking west at Allt na Dunaiche along north bank of stream. An enormously rewarding climb. Rapid descent for scree runners, but allow 8 hours. 928m.

Ben Lawers

Between Killin and Aberfeldy

Massif of seven summits including six Munros dominating north side of Loch Tay are linked by a twisting ridge 12km long that only once falls below 800m. If you're very fit, it's possible to do the lot in a day starting from the north or Glen Lyon side. An easier day of it knocks off Beinn Ghlas then Ben Lawers from visitor centre 5km off the A827. 4/5 hours.

Meall Nan Tarmachan

Between Killin and Aberfeldy

Part of the ridge west of Lawers (above) takes in a Munro and several tops. Not arduous but is immensely impressive. Start 1km further on from NTS visitor centre down 100m track through gate.

Glen Tilt

*Blair Atholl
up to 17km
CIRC
XBIKES
1-B-2*

A walk of variable length in this classic Highland glen, easily accessible from the old Blair Rd off main Blair Atholl road near Bridge of Tilt Hotel, car park by the (very) old bridge. Trail leaflet from park office and local tourist information centres. Fine walking and unspoiled scenery begins only a short distance into the deeply wooded gorge of the River Tilt, but to cover the circular route you have to walk to Gilbert's Bridge (9km return) or the longer trail to Gow's Bridge (17km return). Begin here also the great route into the Cairngorms leading to the Linn of Dee and Braemar, joining the track from Speyside which starts at Feshiebridge or Glenmore Forest.

Glen Affric

*Cannich, Near
Drumnadrochit
5/8 km
CIRC
BIKES
1-B-2*

www.glenaffric.org
Easy short walks are marked and hugely rewarding in this magnificent glen well known as the first stretch in the great east-west route to Kintail and the Falls of Glomach. Starting point of this track into the wilds is at the end of the road at Loch Affric; there are many short and circular trails indicated here. Car park is beyond metal road 2km along forest track towards Affric Lodge (cars not allowed to lodge itself). Track closed in stalking season. Easier walks in famous Affric forest from car park at **Dog Falls**. 7km from Cannich. Waterfalls and spooky tame birds. Good idea to hire bikes at Drumnadrochit or Cannich (01456 415251). Don't miss Glen Affric.

Balquhidder to Brig o' Turk

Central Scotland
18km
XCIRC
XBIKES
2-B-2

Easy amble through the heart of Scotland via Glenfinglas with handy pubs and tea-rooms at either end. Not circular so best to arrange transport. Usually walked starting at Rob Roy graveyard, then Ballimore and past Ben Vane to the reservoir and Brig o' Turk.

Dollar Glen

Dollar
3km + tops
CIRC
XBIKES
1-A-2

The classic fairy glen in Central Scotland, hoaching with water spirits, reeking of ozone and euphoric after rain. Erosion means the path no longer goes deep into the gorge. 20km by A91 from Stirling or 18km from M90 at Kinross junction 6. Start at side of the museum or golf club, or further up road (signed Castle Campbell) at the two car parks, the top one 5 minutes from castle. The castle at head of glen is open 7 days till 6pm (Oct-Mar till 4pm) and has boggling views. There's a circular walk back or take off for the Ochil Tops. There are also first-class walks (the hill trail is more rewarding than the 'Mill Trail') up the glens of the other hillfoot towns, Alva and Tillicoultry.

Rumbling Bridge

Near Dollar
3km
CIRC
XBIKES
1-A-1

An easier short walk in a glen with some-thing of the chasmic experience and added delight of the unique double bridge (built 1713). At the end of one of the walkways under the bridge you are looking into a Scottish jungle landscape as the Romantics imagined. Near Powmill on A977 from Kinross (junction 6, M90) then 2km. Up the road is The Powmill Milkbar serving excellent home-made food. It's 5km west on the A977. Open 7 days till 5pm (6pm weekends). Go after your walk!

Glen Clova

Angus

www.clova.com
Most dramatic of the Angus glens. Most walks from end at Acharn especially west to Glen Doll and the Loops of (Loch) Brandy walk. Enquire at **Glen Clova Hotel** and repair there afterwards (great walkers' pub). Easy, rewarding walks! Check hotel for details.

The Lade Braes

St Andrews
1-A-1

This walk cuts through the town itself following the Kinness Burn. But you are removed from all that! Start at Westport just after the garage on Bridge St or opposite 139 South St. Trailboard and signs. Through Coldshaugh Park (sidespur to Botanics on opposite bank) and the leafy glen and green sward at the edge of this beautiful town. Ends in a duck pond. You pass the back gardens of some very comfortable lives.

Falkland

Fife
3km
CIRC
XBIKES
1-A-2

If you're in Falkland for the Palace or the tearoom, add this amble up an enchanting glen to your day. Go through village then signed Cricket Club for Falkland Estate and School – car park just inside gate (with map) – and gardens are behind it. Glen and refurbished path up the macadam road are obvious. Gushing burn, waterfalls: you even walk behind one! Good café/restaurant in village.

The Big Burn Walk

Golspie
6km
CIRC
XBIKES
1-B-1

A non-taxing, perfect glen walk through lush diverse woodland. Three different entrances including car park marked from A9 near Dunrobin Castle gates but most complete starts beyond Sutherland Arms and Sutherland Stone at the end of the village. Go past derelict mill and under aqueduct following river. A super-nature trail unfolds with ancient tangled trees, meadows, waterfalls, cliffs and wildlife. 3km to falls; return via route to castle woods for all-round intoxication.

The Strath at Dunbeath

Dunbeath
XCIRC
XBIKES
1-B-1

www.dunbeath-heritage.org.uk
The glen or strath so eloquently evoked in Neil Gunn's *Highland River*, a book as much about the geography as the history of his childhood. A path follows the river for many miles. A leaflet from Dunbeath Heritage Centre points out places on the way as well as map on its entire floor. It's a spate river and in summer becomes a trickle; hard to imagine Gunn's salmon odyssey. It's only 500m to the broch, but it's worth going into the hinterland where it becomes quite mystical.

Tweedside

Peebles
5/12km
CIRC
XBIKES
1-A-1

Riverside trail follows the Tweed from town (Hay Lodge Park) past Neidpath Castle through classic Border wooded countryside crossing river either 2.5km out (5km round trip), at Manor Bridge 6km out (Lyne Footbridge, 12km). Pick up *Walking in the Scottish Borders* and other trail guides at tourist information centres. Other good Tweedside walks between Dryburgh Abbey and Bemersyde House grounds and at Newton St Boswells by the golf course.

Failford Gorge

Near Mauchline
3/5km
CIRC
XBIKES
1-A-1

Woody gorge of the River Ayr. Start from bridge at Ayr end of village on B743 Ayr-Mauchline road (4km Mauchline). Easy, marked trail. Pub in village great for ale (they brew their own 'Windie Goat'!) and local craic but better for food is the **Sorn Inn** east of Mauchline. Very pleasant.

Glen Lednock

Near Comrie
3/5km
CIRC
XBIKES
1-A-1

Walk from Comrie or take car further up to monument, or drive further into glen to reservoir (9km) for more open walks. From town take right off main A85 (to Lochearnhead) at **Deil's Cauldron** restaurant. Walk and Deil's Cauldron (waterfall and gorge) are signed after 250m. Walk takes less than an hour and emerges on road near Lord Melville's monument (climb for great views back towards Crieff; about 25 minutes). Other walks up slopes to left after you emerge from the tree-lined gorge road. There's also the start of a hike up Ben Chonzie, 6km up the glen at Coishavachan, an easy Munro (931m), with a good path and great views, especially to the northwest.

Gannochy Bridge & Rocks of Solitude

Near Edzell
2km
XCIRC
XBIKES
1-A-1

2km north of village on B966 to Fettercairn. There's a lay-by after bridge and a wooden door on left (you're in the grounds of the Burn House). Through it is another world and a path above the rocky gorge of the River North Esk (1km). Huge stone ledges over dark pools. You don't have to be alone (well, maybe you do).

Near Taynuilt

Taynuilt
10km
CIRC
BIKES
1-A-1

A walk (recommended by readers) combining education with recreation. Start behind Bonawe Ironworks and go along the riverside to suspension bridge and thence to Inverawe Smokehouse (open to the public; café). All very nice. Best not to park in Bonawe car park (for HS visitors, and it closes at 6pm).

Glen Trool

Near Newton Stewart

A simple non-climbing, well marked route round Loch Trool. A circular 8km but with many options. And a caff.

Kintra

Islay
XCIRC
XBIKES
2-B-2

On Bowmore-Port Ellen road take Oa turnoff: then Kintra signed 7km. Park in old farmyard by campsite. A fabulous beach runs in opposite direction and a notable golf course behind it. This walk leads along north coast of the Mull of Oa, an area of diverse beauty, sometimes pastoral, sometimes wild, with a wonderful shoreline. Many great picnic spots.

The Bullers of Buchan

Near Peterhead

8km south of Peterhead on A975 road to/from Cruden Bay. Park and walk 100m to cottages. To the north is the walk to Longhaven Nature Reserve, a continuation of the dramatic cliffs and more seabird city. The Bullers is at start of walk, a sheer-sided 'hole' 75m deep with an outlet to the sea through a natural arch. Walk round the edge of it, looking down on layers of birds (who might try to dive-bomb you away from their nests); it's a wonder of nature on an awesome coast. Take great care (and a head for heights).

Cape Wrath & The Cliffs of Clo Mor

✓ ✓

Cape Wrath

www.capewrath.org.uk
Britain's most northwesterly point reached by ferry from 1km off the A838 4km south of Durness by Cape Wrath Hotel; 10-minute crossing and 40-minute minibus ride to Cape. Ferry holds 12 and runs May-Sep (01971 511343 for times). At 280m Clo Mor are the highest cliffs in UK; 4km round trip from Cape. MoD range – access may be restricted. In other direction, the 28km to Kinlochbervie is one of Britain's most wild and wonderful coastal walks. Beaches include Sandwood. While in this North West area: Smoo Cave 2km east of Durness.

Old Man Of Stoer

Near Lochinver
1-B-2

The easy, exhilarating walk to the dramatic 70km sandstone sea stack. Start from lighthouse off unclassified road 14km north Lochinver. Park and follow sheep tracks; cliffs are high and steep. 7km round trip; 2/3 hours. Then find the Secret Beach.

Rockcliffe to Kippford

South West
1-A-2

An easy and can-be-circular stroll along the 'Scottish Riviera' through woodland near the shore (2km) past the 'Mote of Mark', a Dark Age hill fort with views to Rough Island. The better clifftop walk is in the other direction to Castlehillpoint. Good teashop in Rockcliffe.

St Abbs Head

5-10km
CIRC
XBIKES
1-B-2

Some of the most dramatic coastal scenery in Southern Scotland, scary in a wind, rhapsodic on a blue summer's day. Extensive wildlife reserve and trails through coastal hills and vales to cliffs. Cars go as far as lighthouse, but best park at visitor centre near farm on St Abbs village road 3km from A1107 to Eyemouth and follow route. Very nice caff here.

Applecross

Applecross Bay

Far peninsula marvellous for many reasons including staying alive and eating out, but there are fine walks in and around the foreshore of the bay including river and woodland strolls. All detailed in a 'scenic walks' leaflet available locally.

Singing Sands

Ardnamurchan
10km ret
XCIRC
BIKES
1-B-1

2km north of Acharacle, signed for Arevegaig. 3km to Arevegaig and park before wooden bridge (gate may be locked). Cross the wooden bridge, following the track round the side of Kentra

Bay. Follow the signs for Gorteneorn, and walk through forest track and woodland to beach. As you pound the sands they should 'sing' to you whilst you bathe in the beautiful views of Rum, Eigg, Muck and Skye (and just possibly the sea). Check at the tourist information centre for directions and other walks booklet. 'Beware unexploded mines', it says. Mmm!

East From Cullen

Moray Coast
8KM
XCIRC
XBIKES
1-A-1

This is the same walk mentioned with reference to Sunnyside, a golden beach with a fabulous ruined castle (Findlater) that might be your destination. There's a track east along from harbour. 2 hours return. Superb coastline.

Crovie-Troup Head

Moray Coast

Another Moray Coast classic that takes in the extraordinary cliff-clinging village of Crovie and bird-stacked cliffs of the headland. Start at car park and viewpoint above Crovie 15km east of Banff off B9031. Park then walk to end of village and from there follow the path to Troup Head. 5km return.

The South Sutor

Cromarty
5km
CIRC
XBIKES
1-A-1

The walk, known locally as 'The 100 Steps' though there are a few more than that, from Cromarty village round the tip of the south promontory at the narrow entrance to the Cromarty Firth. East of the village; the coastal path hugs the shoreline then ascends through woodland to the headland. Good bench! Go further to the top car park and viewpoint panel. Return by road. There may be dolphins!

The Chain Walk

Elie
2-B-2

Unique and adventurous headland scramble at the west end of Elie (and Earlsferry). Go to end of the road then by the path skirting the golf course towards headland. Hand- and footholds carved into the rock with chains that you use to haul yourself up. Emerge by Shell Bay Caravan Park. Watch the tide; and don't go alone.

Cock of Arran

Lochranza
2-B-2

This round trip starts in the moors but descends to a breathtaking coastal trail past some interesting spots. Great for twitchers, ramblers and fossils (strong boots needed)! Approx 8km (5 hours) from village. Take a picnic.

All open to women, non-members and inexpert players. See VisitScotland's Official Guide to Golf in Scotland, available from tourist information centres.

Machrie

✓

Isle of Islay
01496 302310

www.machrie.com
7km Port Ellen. Worth going to Islay just for the golf. The Machrie (Golf) Hotel is sparse but convenient. Old-fashioned course to be played by feel and instinct. Splendid, sometimes windy isolation with a warm bar and restaurant at the end. The notorious 17th, 'Iffrin' (it means Hell), vortex shaped from the dune system of marram and close-cropped grass, is one of many great holes. 18 holes.

Macrihanish

✓

By Campbeltown
01586 810213

www.machgolf.com
Amongst the dunes and links of the glorious 8km stretch of the Machrihanish Beach. The Atlantic provides thunderous applause for your triumphs over a challenging course. 9/18 holes.

Southerness

✓

Solway Firth
01387 880677

www.southernessgolfclub.com
25km south of Dumfries by A710. A championship course on links on the silt flats of the Firth. Despite its prestige, visitors do get on. Start times available 10-12pm and 2-4pm. Few courses as good as this at this price (under £50 a round). Under the wide Solway sky, it's pure – southerness. 18 holes.

Rosemount

✓

Blairgowrie
01250 872622

www.theblairgowriegolfclub.co.uk
Off A93, south of Blairgowrie. Pampered and well-managed course in the middle of green Perthshire. Easier to get on (most days) than Gleneagles and cheaper (though not at weekends). 18 holes.

Boat of Garten

✓

01479 831282

www.boatgolf.com
Challenging, picturesque course in town where ospreys have been known to wheel overhead. Has been called the 'Gleneagles of the North'; certainly the best around but not for novices. 18 holes.

Tain & Brora

✓

*01862 892314
&
01408 621911*

Two northern courses that are a delight to play on. Tain designed by Tom Morris in 1890. Brora stunning with good clubhouse; coos on the course. With Royal Dornoch, they're a roving-golfer must.

Glencruitten

*Oban
01631 562868*

www.obangolf.com
Picturesque course on the edge of town. Head south (A816) from Argyll Sq, bearing left at church. Course is signed. Quite tricky with many blind holes. Can get busy, so phone first. 18 holes.

Gairloch

*Gairloch
01445 712407*

www.gairlochgolfclub.com
As you come into town from the south on A832, it looks over the bay and down to a perfect, pink, sandy beach. Small clubhouse with honesty box out of hours. Not the world's most agonising course; on a clear day with views to Skye, you can forget agonising over anything. 9 holes.

Harris Golf Club

*Scarista,
Isle of Harris
01859 550226*

www.harrisgolf.com
Phone number is for the captain, but no need to phone: just turn up on the road between Tarbert and Rodel and leave £10 in the box. First tee commands one of the great views in golf and throughout this basic, but testing course, you look out to sea over Scarista beach and bay. Sunset may put you off your swing.

New Galloway

01644 420737

www.nggc.co.uk
Local course on south edge of this fine wee toon. Almost all on a slope but affording great views of Loch Ken and the Galloway Forest behind. No bunkers and only nine short holes, but exhilarating play. Easy on, except Sun. Just turn up.

Minto & Vertish Hill

*Denholm
& Hawick
01450 870220
&
01450 372293*

www.mintogolf.co.uk
Minto is 9km east of Hawick in spacious parkland in Teviot valley. Best holes 3rd, 12th and 16th. Vertish Hill is a more challenging hill course. Both among the best in Borders. 18 holes; best holes 2nd and 18th. An excellent guide to all Borders courses is available from tourist information centres: *Freedom of the Fairways.*

Taymouth Castle

*Kenmore
01887 830228*

www.scotland-golf.co.uk
Spacious green acres around the enigmatic empty hulk of the castle. Well-tended and organised course between A827 to Aberfeldy and the river. Inexpensive, and guests at the Kenmore Hotel get special rate. 18 holes.

Gifford

01620 810591

www.giffordgolfclub.com
Dinky inland course on edge of a dinky village, bypassed by the queue for the big East Lothian courses and a guarded secret among the regulars. Generally ok, but phone starter for available. 9 holes.

Strathpeffer

01997 421219

www.strathpeffergolf.co.uk
Very hilly course full of character and exhilarating Highland views. Small-town friendliness. You play up there with the gods and other old codgers. 18 holes.

Elgin

01343 542338

www.elgingolfclub.com
1km from town on A941 Perth road. Many memorable holes on moorland/parkland course in an area where links may lure you to the coast (Nairn, Lossiemouth). 18 holes.

Durness

01971 511364

www.durnessgolfclub.org
The most northerly golf course on mainland UK, on the wild headland by Balnakeil Bay, looking over to Faraid Head. The last hole is 'over the sea'. Only open since 1988, it's already got cult status. 2km west of Durness.

Rothesay

01700 503554

www.rothesaygolfclub.com
Sloping course with breathtaking views of Clyde. Visitors welcome. What could be finer than taking the train from Glasgow to Wemyss Bay for the ferry over and 18 holes. Finish up with fish 'n' chips at the West End on the way home.

Traigh

Arisaig
01445 712407

www.traighgolf.co.uk
A830 Fort William-Mallaig road, 2km north Arisaig. Pronounced 'try' - and you may want to. The islands are set out like stones in the sea around you and there are nine hilly holes of fun. Has been called 'the most beautiful nine holes in the world'.

The Borders

The Borders with its gentle hills, river tracks and low urbanisation is paving the cycleway for mountain biking and more leisurely family pursuits. Good linkage and signage; many routes, eg the Four Abbeys, Tweed Cycleway, Borderloop and individual trails. Guides from tourist information centres for almost all towns. Ample choice for all abilities and ages.

Speyside Way
Craigellachie-Ballindalloch

20km
Can be CIRC

Cycling part of the Speyside Way, with great views; flat and no cars. Passes distilleries. Circular return on minor roads. START Craigellachie by rangers' office.

Forth & Clyde Canal Glasgow-Falkirk Wheel

55km

East out of the city, urban at first then nice in the Kelvin Valley; Kilsyth Hills to the north. Falkirk Wheel should be seen. START The Maryhill Locks, Maryhill Rd.

Glentrool

*Near
Newton Stewart
15km
Can be CIRC*

Two routes from visitor centre. Deep in forest and well signed. Briefly joins public road. 7 Stanes sections can be difficult. START Glentrool visitor centre off A714. Bike hire at Kirroughtree and network of trails listed from here.

Edinburgh Trails

*12km/
VARIOUS
CIRC*

Edinburgh streets can be a nightmare for cyclists and there's lots of uphill graft. But there is a vast network of cycle and towpaths especially north of the New Town. Another good run is to Balerno from Union Canal towpath in lower Gilmore Place; end at Balerno High School.

The Trossachs

Near Aberfoyle
& Callander
11km
Can be CIRC

www.lochlomond-trossachs.org
Many low-level lochside trails. Consult tourist information centres. Nice run is Loch Ard Circle from Aberfoyle going west (signed Inversnaid Scenic Route).

Loch An Eilean

Near Aviemore
20km
CIRC

Lots of bike tracks here in the Rothiemurchus Forrest. This one goes past one of Scotland's most beautiful lochs and you can go further to Loch Insh via Feshiebridge and around Glen Feshie. Probably best to get a route leaflet at visitor centre (loch car park and Coylumbridge). The Outsider Festival uses this route.
START signed from B970 at Coylumbridge.

Cumbrae

Take the ferry from Largs to beautiful Cumbrae Island. There are four or five routes around the island. One is a stiff pull to a great viewpoint while others stick to sea level. Consult the leaflet from local tourist information centre. All island roads are quiet.

7 Stanes

*Borders &
South West*

www.7stanes.gov.uk
Ambitious and hugely popular network of
bike trails, some still under construction.
Includes Glentress/Tweed Valley (below),
Newcastleton, Forest of Ae, Dalbeattie,
Mabie, Glentrool (above), and
Kirroughtree (above). Routes at all levels.
Good signage; information from local
tourist information centres.

Glentress Forest

Near Peebles

www.thehubintheforest.co.uk
Specially constructed trails for all levels,
plenty of flowing descents and drops.
Well signed and well used. Great café. **7
Stanes** route starts nearby at Traquair.

Clatteringshaws

*Near Glentrool
25km
CIRC*

Various routes around Clatteringshaws
Loch in the Galloway Forest and Hills.
Most are easy, but some serious climbs
and descents. Tearoom in visitor centre.

Glen Tanner

*Deeside
25km
CIRC*

www.royal-deeside.org.uk
Good way to encounter this beautiful
glen in the shadow of Mount Keen. Quite
difficult in places.
START Tombae on the B976 opposite
junction of A97 and A93.

Great Glen

XCIRC

Easy start on Caledonian Canal towpath,
then hilly with long climbs. Great views.
START Neptune's Staircase at Banavie.

Glenfernate-Blair Atholl

*Perthshire
& Angus
25km
CIRC*

Beautiful Highland trail takes in forests,
lochs and Glen Tilt. Mainly rough track.
Directions on tourist information leaflets.
START On the A924 14km east of
Pitlochrie, 500m east of school.

Scotland's seas are primal soup, full of life and world-class sites as hard-core divers already know. The East Coast can be tricky if the wind is blowing from the north or east, therefore the West Coast is preferable (the further north the better).

Thanks to the Gulf Stream it's not cold, even without a dry suit, and once you're down it's like flying through the Botanics (says my friend Tim Maguire).

All West Coast sea lochs are good for general wildlife diving. So when you see all those crazies walking into the sea, remember, they may know something that you don't.

THE WEST COAST
The Outer Hebrides

Excellent with fantastic visibility especially off the west coast of Harris where you can plop in virtually anywhere.

St Kilda

Offers the best diving in the UK, but it's the hardest to get to. On the edge of the Continental Shelf and the whale migration route, it has huge drop-offs and upwellings of life. Book boat and board well in advance.

Loch Creran

North of Oban

Long sea loch now designated a Marine Special Area of Conservation for its biogenic reefs (the most important site for 'serpulid reefs' in Europe.

Oban

Scuba central with lots of sites and easy access to the isles. Charter a boat and search for scallops in The Garvellach or dive the wrecks in the Sound of Mull. Somewhere off Tobermory there is reputedly one of Scotland's most enigmatic wrecks, a Spanish galleon. Easier to find are dolphins off the coasts of Islay and Tiree.

The Summer Isles

From Ullapool. Wrecks, lee shores and unpolluted waters.

THE EAST COAST
St Abbs Head

Accessible from the shore or by boat from Eyemouth, a marine reserve, so leave the lobsters alone. The spectacular Cathedral Rock is encrusted with green and yellow dead men's fingers and in Aug/Sep is a sanctuary for breeding fish (this cathedral is as beautiful as St Giles and is distinctly non-denominational). Nearby shore-based diving at Dunbar is shallow, safe and simple.

The Isle of May

Across the Forth; more advanced. Take a boat from Anstruther. Main site is Piccadilly Circus, a central atrium fed by gullies, full of friendly seals.

ORKNEY
Scapa Flow

www.scapaflow.co.uk
World-famous underwater burial site where the Germans scuttled their fleet in 1918. Think Gaudalcanal, but colder. Although the scrappies have been in, three battleships and four light cruisers remain among other wrecks. Most lie in 20-40m deep, so not so dark and dangerous but plan carefully. Still majorly eerie!

A surprise for the sceptical: Scotland has some of the best surfing beaches in Europe. Forget the bronzed beach boys and lemon-bleached hair, surfing in Scotland is titanium-lined, rubber and balaclavas, and you get an ice-cream head even encased in the latest technology. The main season is Sep-Dec.

THE WEST COAST
Isle of Lewis

Probably the best of the lot. Go north of Stornoway, north of Barvas, north of just about anywhere. Leave the A857 and your day job behind. Not the most scenic of sites, but the waves have come a long way, further than you have. Derek at Hebridean Surf Holidays (01851 705862) will tell you when and where to go.

Isle of Tiree

Exposed to all the Atlantic swells, gorgeous little Tiree ain't just great for windsurfing. Stay at Millhouse, self-catering hostel (01879 220435); good facilities.

Macrihanish

Near Campbeltown at the foot of the Mull of Kintyre. Long strand to choose from. Clan Skates in Glasgow (0141 339 6523) usually has an up-to-date satellite map and a idea of both the west and (nearest to central belt) Pease Bay (see opposite).

THE NORTH COAST
Thurso

Surf City. Well not quite, but it's a good base to find your own waves. Especially to the east of town at Dunnet Bay – a 5km-long beach with excellent reefs at the north end. They say it has to be the best right-hand breaking wave on the planet! When it ain't breaking, go west to...

Melvich & Strathy Bay

Near Bettyhill on the North Coast halfway between Tongue and Thurso on the A836. From here to Cape Wrath the power and quality of the waves detonating on the shore have justified comparisons with Hawaii. And then there's Brimsness.

Wick

On the Thurso road at Ackergill to the south of Sinclair's Bay. Find the ruined castle and taking care, clamber down the gully to the beach. A monumental reef break, you are working against the backdrop of the decaying ruin drenched in history, spume and romance.

THE EAST COAST
Rattray Head

Between Peterhead & Fraserburgh

5km off A90. Hostel/B&B 300m from secret 15km beach with cool surf. (B&B 01346 532236.)

Nigg Bay

Just south of Aberdeen (not to be confused with Nigg across from Cromarty) and off the vast beach at Lunan Bay between Arbroath and Montrose. There's 4 spots around Fraserburgh ('the broch').

Pease Bay

South of Dunbar near Cockburnspath on the A1. The nearest surfie heaven to the capital. The caravan site has parking and toilets. Very consistent surf here and therefore very popular.

These galleries are the best places where tourists can buy typical Scottish work. There are also many other galleries which are considered to be important and you can find them in other sections in Scotland the Best.

McEwan Gallery

Near Ballater, Deeside

www.mcewangallery.com
A surprising place but for many years this cottage gallery has been dealing in 19th/20th century, mainly Scottish art. They wrote the book! Summer exhibitions, but open all year 11am-5pm (Sun 2-5pm). Winter hours call (01339 755429). 300m up A939 Tomintoul road.

The Lost Gallery

Middle of Nowhere, Aberdeenshire

www.lostgallery.co.uk
Signed from Bellabeg on A944 near Strathon village. 3km up farm road, then another 3km on rough track to a fab studio/gallery in Cairngorms farmhouse with varied work by contemporary Scots and the owner Peter Goodfellow. All year 11am-5pm. Closed Tue. (Phone 01975 651287 if you get... lost.)

Browns Gallery

Tain

Off Main St. Surprising repository of great contemporary Scottish art with regular exhibitions by notable artists like John Byrne, Calvin Colvin, Neil Macpherson. They must like this guy. Whole new gallery space '07. It does Tain proud. Mon-Sat 10am-5pm.

Kilmorack Gallery

Near Beauly
01463 783230

www.kilmorackgallery.co.uk
On A831 for Struy and Cannich 5km southwest of town. Pleasant and serious gallery in converted church by the road. Significant exhibitions of mainly Highland artists including the ubiquitous James Hawkins. Some sculpture.

Castle Gallery

Inverness

www.castlegallery.co.uk

On road up to castle amid many restaurants, another Highland gallery that takes itself quite seriously. Changing exhibitions. Mon-Sat 9am-5pm.

Strathearn Gallery

32 West Street, Crieff

www.strathearn-gallery.com

(On Main St). Accessible and affordable. The Maguires do know what you like. Fine and applied arts; lots of ceramics. 7 days till 5pm (Thu-Sat in winter).

Solas Gallery

Gairloch

www.solasgallery.co.uk

Flowerdale Bay by the Old Inn as you come into Gairloch from south. Original work - painting, ceramics - by West Highland artists. Nice space. Easter-Oct.

Plockton Gallery

Innes Street, Plockton

www.painting-in-plockton.co.uk

Opposite Plockton Inn. Two floors, lots of wall space for summer exhibitions including some significant artists. Summer only 10am-10pm.

Gallery An Talla Dearg

Eilean Iarmain, Sleat, Skye

True Gaelic corner of the world. This gallery open in summer adjacent legendary hotel and bar. Artists that we tourists like: Laurence Broderick (who does otters) and Pam Carter (who does the business).

Finsbay Gallery

Golden Road, South Harris

www.witb.co.uk/links/finsbay.htm

Wonderful windy road down east coast of South Harris. This cute gallery showing mainly Hebridean artists. Another gallery (Skoon)/café nearby. Mon-Sat 10am-5pm (winter Thu only).

St Andrews Fine Art

www.st-andrewsfineart.co.uk
Crowded walls of Scottish art from 1800-present. Includes some good work from kent contemporaries. Peploe-Redpath and their chums. Closed Sun.

Kranenburg & Fowler Fine Arts

Star Brae &
Stevenson Street,
Oban
01631 562303

www.kranenburg-fowler.com
Geoff and Jan source work from artists that ranges from the polite to the interesting. Small group of regular exhibitors and others. Mon-Sat 9.30am-5.30pm. Sun when exhibition 12noon-4pm.

Whitehouse Gallery

St Mary's Street,
Kirkcudbright

Self-proclaimed artists' town (Hornel, Jessie M. King and others did live and work here). Supports local artists. Worth a browse. Tue-Sat, 10am-5pm.

Morven Gallery

Barvas,
Isle of Lewis

www.morvengallery.com
Coast road just north of Barabhas 30km from Callanish and those stones. Janice Scott's excellent farm steading kind of gallery with well-selected work, mainly local. Painting, tapestry, ceramics and fab original knits. Baking. Good tearoom. Apr-Oct 10am-5.30pm. Closed Sun.

Scottish Sculpture Workshops

Lumsden
01464 861372

www.ssw.org.uk
Main street of ribbon town on A97 near Alford and Huntly. Not a place to see work for sale (mainly commissions), but work being made. They also look after the sculpture garden at Alford end of the street by the school. Workshops open all year. Mon-Fri 9am-5pm.

Stenton Gallery

Stenton,
East Lothian

Deep in the green undulations of the East Lothian countryside but not far from the A1 on the B6370 from Dunbar round-about. 10 years established, surprisingly extensive gallery with eclectic range of contemporary Scottish artists. 11am-5pm. Closed Thu.

ALSO...

The Glasgow Art Fair

0141 552 6027

www.glasgowartfair.com
The Scottish marketplace for contemporary art. Mainly home-grown but London galleries with Scottish connections. Held in mid April in pavilions in George Square. Excellent refreshments.

The Art School Degree Shows

Edinburgh,
Glasgow,
Duncan Of
Jordanstone,
Dundee

Work from final-year art-school students. Discover the Bellanys, Howsons, Douglas Gordons and Simon Starlings of the future. Two-week exhibitions after manic first nights (mid Jun).

Eden Court Theatre

Inverness
01463 234234

www.eden-court.co.uk
A theatre complex which has always made a vital contribution to the cultural life of the Highlands. Reopened after a lengthy, major refurbishment; it is now probably the best multi-theatre facility in Scotland.

Dundee Rep

Tay Square,
Dundee
01382 223530

www.dundeerep.co.uk
Cornerstone of Dundee's cultural quarter (with DCA). Houses Scotland's only rep company. Ambitious programme. Anyone into contemporary Scottish drama comes here. Good café.

Bowhill Little Theatre

Bowhill House
Near Selkirk
01750 22204

www.bowhilllittletheatre.org
Tiny (72-seat) theatre off the courtyard below Bowhill House. Intermittent programme (check first), but always delightful, especially with supper afterwards in Courtyard Restaurant (phone to book).

Eastgate

Main Street,
Peebles
01721 725777

www.eastgatearts.com
Beautiful, state-of-the-art wee theatre clamped on to the back of a church (by eminent architect Richard Murphy) at Galashiels end of main street. Eclectic programming. Expect everything! Caff and excellent restaurant adjacent.

Pitlochry Theatre

Pitlochry
01796 484626

www.pitlochry.org.uk
Modern rep theatre across the river from main street usually performs six plays on different nights of the week. Well-chosen programme of classics and popular works: the 500-seat theatre is often full. Mixed Sunday concerts and foyer fringe events. Coffee bar and restaurant menu.

Byre Theatre

Abbey Street /
South Street,
St Andrews
01334 476288

www.byretheatre.com
A lottery-funded major reconstruction. Great auditorium and café-bar. Major social hub for town and gown. Eclectic programme of theatre, music, comedy. Prince William, however, has moved on.

Cumbernauld Theatre

01236 732887

www.cumbernauldtheatre.co.uk
On a rise overlooking A80; follow signs for Cumbernauld House. Bar/café-restaurant and theatre (in the round) with a mixed programme of one-nighters and short runs of mainly Scottish touring companies. Also concerts, drama workshops and kids' programmes.

The Wynd

Melrose
01896 820028

www.thewynd.com
100-seater arts venue which regularly entertains locals and Edinburgh folk. From classic Ibsen and musicals to folk, jazz, dance and film. Intimate atmosphere in an intimate town.

Campbeltown Picture House

01586 553899

www.weepictures.co.uk
Cinema Paradiso on the Kintyre peninsula. Lovingly preserved Art Deco shrine to the movies, first opened 1913. Mainly first-run films. To see a film here and emerge onto the esplanade of Campbeltown Loch is to experience the lost magic of a night at the pictures.

The New Picture House

North Street,
St Andrews
01334 473509

www.nphcinema.co.uk
'New' means 1931 and it hasn't changed too much, as generations of students remember fondly. Mainly first-run flicks; Oct-May, a programme of late-night cult/art movies.

Dun Caan

Raasay
10km
XCIRC
XBIKES
2-B-2

Still one of my favourite island walks – to the flat top of a magic hill, the one you see from most of the east coast of Skye. Take the ferry, ask for route from Inverarish. Go via old iron mine; looks steep when you get over the ridge, but it's a dawdle. And amazing.

The Lost Glen

Harris
12km RET
XCIRC
XBIKES
2-B-2

Take B887 west from Tarbert almost to the end (where at Hushinish there's a good beach, maybe a sunset), but go right before the Big House (signed Chliostair Power Station). Park here or further in and walk to dam (3km from road). Take right track round reservoir and left around the upper loch. Over the brim you arrive in a wide, wild glen; an overhang 2km ahead is said to have the steepest angle in Europe. Go quietly; if you don't see deer and eagles here, you're making too much noise on the grass.

Carsaig

Mull
15/20km RET
XCIRC
XBIKES
2-B-2

In south of island, 7km from A849 Fionnphort-Craignure road near Pennyghael. Two walks start at pier: going left towards Lochbuie for a spectacular coastal/woodland walk past Adnunan Stack (7km); or right towards the imposing headland where, under the cliffs, the Nuns' Cave was a shelter for nuns evicted from Iona during the Reformation. Nearby is a quarry whose stone was used to build Iona Abbey and much further on (9km Carsaig), at Malcolm's Point, the extraordinary Carsaig Arches carved by wind and sea.

Cock of Arran

Lochranza
11km
CIRC
XBIKES

Turn right at church and follow signs. 8/9km circular walk into Glen Chalmadale and high into moorland (260m), then drops down to magnificent shoreline. Here eagles catch the updraft and peregrines lose it. Divers and ducks share the shore with seals. About 1km from where you meet the shore, look for Giant Centipede fossil trail. Further on at opening of wall pace 350 steps and turn left up to Ossian's Cave. Path crosses Fairy Dell Burn and eventually comes out at Lochranza Bay. Allow 5/6 hours and stout boots (good walk descending from youth hostel).

Colonsay

12 + 6km
XCIRC
BIKES
1-A-2

From hotel or the quay, walk to Colonsay House and its lush, overgrown intermingling of native plants and exotics (8km round trip); or to the priory on Oronsay, the smaller island. 6km to 'the Strand' (you might get a lift with the postman) then cross at low tide, with enough time (at least 2 hours) to walk to the ruins. Allow longer if you want to climb the easy peak of Ben Oronsay. Tide tables at hotel. Nice walk also from Kiloran Beach to Balnahard Beach – farm track 12km return.

The Trotternish Ridge

Skye
30km
XCIRC
XBIKES

website.lineone.net/~trotternish/walking.html

The 30km Highland walk which takes in the Quirang and the Old Man of Stoer (see next page for both) offers many shorter walks without climbing or scrambling as well as the whole monty (a 2-day hike).

The Old Man Of Stoer

Skye
5km
XCIRC
XBIKES
2-B-2

The enigmatic basalt finger visible from the Portree-Staffin road (A855). Start from car park on left, 12km from Portree. There's a well-defined path through woodland and then towards the cliffs and a steep climb up the grassy slope to the pinnacle which towers 165ft tall. Great views over Raasay to the mainland. Lots of space and rabbits and birds who make the most of it.

The Quirang

Skye
6km
XCIRC
XBIKES
2-B-2

The strange formations have names (eg the Table, the Needle, the Prison) and it's possible to walk round all of them. Start of the path from the car park is easy. At the first saddle, take the second scree slope to the Table, rather than the first. When you get to the Needle, the path to the right between two giant pinnacles is the easiest of the three options. From the top you can see the Hebrides. This place is supernatural; anything could happen. So be careful.

Scorrybreac

Skye
3km
CIRC
XBIKES
1-A-1

A much simpler prospect than the above and more quietly spectacular but mentioned here because anyone could do it; it's only 3km and it's more or less in Portree. Head for Cuillin Hills Hotel off Staffin Rd out of town. Shoreline path signed just below hotel. Passes 'Black Rock', where once Bonnie Prince Charlie left for Raasay, and continues round hill. Nice views back to the bright lights of Portree.

Hoy

Orkney
20/25km
CIRC
MT BIKES
2-B-2

There are innumerable walks on the scattered Orkney Islands and on Hoy itself; on a good day you can get round the north part of the island and see some of the most dramatic coastal scenery anywhere. A passenger ferry leaves Stromness two or three times a day and takes 30 minutes. Make tracks north or south from junction near pier and use free Hoy brochure from tourist information centre so as not to miss the landmarks, the bird sanctuaries and the Old Man himself.

Corryvreckan

Jura
6/24km
XCIRC
XBIKES
2-C-2

The whirlpool in the Gulf of Corryvreckan is notorious. Between Jura and Scarba; to see it go to far north of Jura. From end of the road at Ardlussa (25km Craighouse, the village), there's a rough track to Lealt then a walk (a local may drive you) of 12km to Kinuachdrach, then a further walk of 3km. Phenomenon best seen at certain states of tide. There are boat trips from Crinan and Oban – details from tourist information centres. Consult hotel and get the walk guide.

Sgurr An

Eigg

Unmissable treat if you're on Eigg. Take to the big ridge. Not a hard pull, and extraordinary views and island perspective from the top.

Scot land the best

'The only guide worth a damn'
The Scotsman

Order now and save 40%!

To order your complete copy of *Scotland the Best* at the special price of £8.99 (RRP £14.99) call the HarperCollins Hotline on: 0870 787 1732 and quote Dept 276K.

Or write to:

   Mail Order Dept 276K,
   HarperCollins Publishers,
   Westerhill Road,
   Bishopsbriggs,
   Glasgow G64 2QT

enclosing a cheque made payable to HarperCollins Publishers.

Free P & P for all UK orders.
Please allow 21 days for delivery.